SOCCER
RECORD
BREAKERS

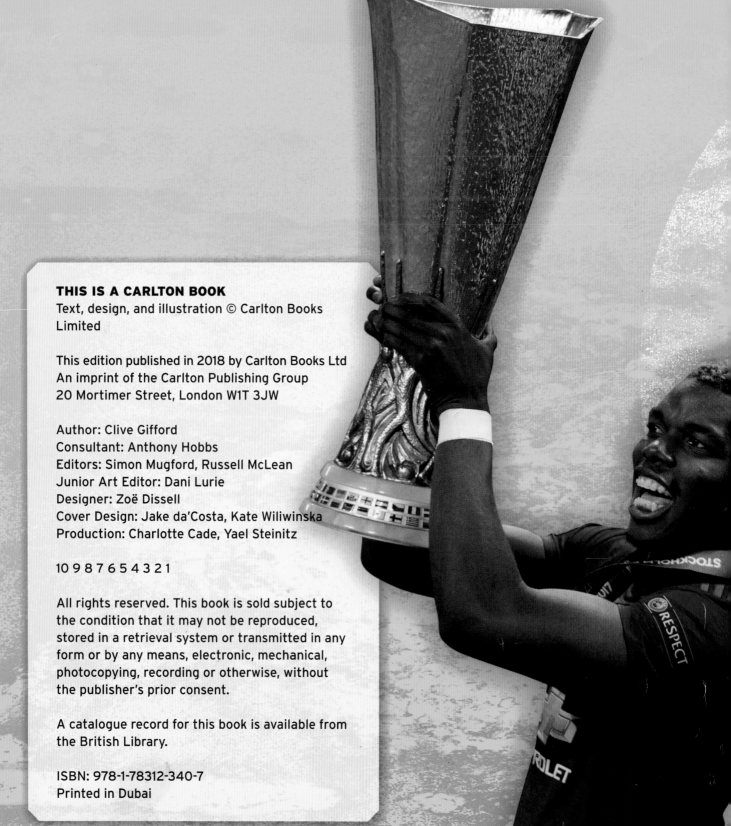

THIS IS A CARLTON BOOK
Text, design, and illustration © Carlton Books
Limited

This edition published in 2018 by Carlton Books Ltd
An imprint of the Carlton Publishing Group
20 Mortimer Street, London W1T 3JW

Author: Clive Gifford
Consultant: Anthony Hobbs
Editors: Simon Mugford, Russell McLean
Junior Art Editor: Dani Lurie
Designer: Zoë Dissell
Cover Design: Jake da'Costa, Kate Wiliwinska
Production: Charlotte Cade, Yael Steinitz

10 9 8 7 6 5 4 3 2 1

A catalogue record for this book is available from
the British Library.

ISBN: 978-1-78312-340-7
Printed in Dubai

SOCCER RECORD BREAKERS

GOAL SCORERS!

TROPHY WINNERS!

SOCCER LEGENDS!

CLIVE GIFFORD

CARLTON KiDS

CONTENTS

FOOTBALL RECORD BREAKERS

★ ★ ★ ★ ★ ★

NOTE: the facts and records in this book are accurate up to and including the 2017 Champions League final.

THE GLOBAL GAME

Football is the world's most popular team sport, with hundreds of millions of players and even more fans watching games live, on TV or via the Internet. It is played all over the globe, with every nation having its own football association to organize competitions and teams. These football associations are members of bodies called confederations, which run continental competitions such as the UEFA Champions League and the CONCACAF Gold Cup.

FIFA

Full name: Fédération Internationale de Football Association
Headquarters: Zurich, Switzerland

Founded in 1904 in Paris, FIFA runs the world game. It awards the rights to host major global tournaments such as the Under-17 World Cup, the Confederations Cup and most notably the men's and women's World Cups. The FIFA World Cup was set up during the reign of FIFA's longest-serving president, Frenchman Jules Rimet (president from 1921 to 1954).

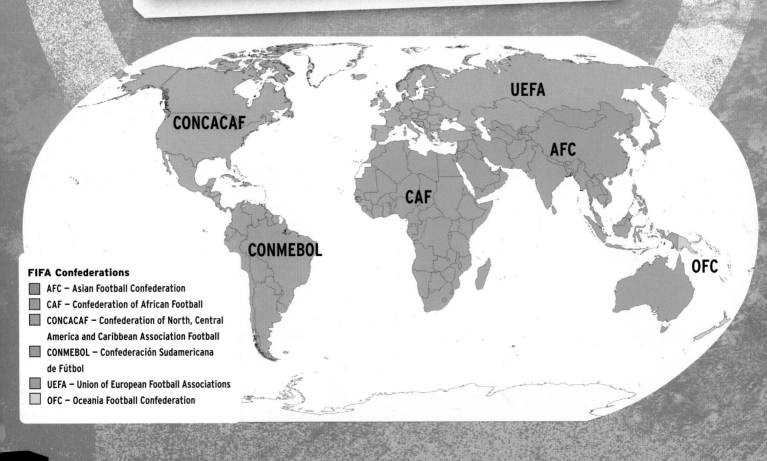

FIFA Confederations

- **AFC** – Asian Football Confederation
- **CAF** – Confederation of African Football
- **CONCACAF** – Confederation of North, Central America and Caribbean Association Football
- **CONMEBOL** – Confederación Sudamericana de Fútbol
- **UEFA** – Union of European Football Associations
- **OFC** – Oceania Football Confederation

AFC

Full name: Asian Football Confederation
Headquarters: Kuala Lumpur, Malaysia
Formed in 1954 in the Philippines, the AFC began with 12 members but now has 47 nations ranging from the Northern Mariana Islands with a population of less than 60,000 to China with its 1.4 billion inhabitants. Kazakhstan was a member between 1998 and 2002 before joining UEFA. The AFC is responsible for organizing the Asian Champions League for clubs and the men's and women's Asian Cup for national teams.

 ## CONMEBOL

Full name: Confederación Sudamericana de Fútbol
Headquarters: Luque, Paraguay
Formed in 1916, CONMEBOL is the oldest football confederation. It also has the fewest members with just 10 associations, but these include powerhouses such as Argentina and Brazil. CONMEBOL members have won the Confederations Cup five times and the FIFA World Cup nine times (and been runners-up a further five times). The confederation organizes the highly competitive Copa Libertadores for leading South American clubs and the Copa América for national teams.

 ## CAF

Full name: Confederation of African Football
Headquarters: 6th of October City, Egypt
In 1957, South Africa, Sudan, Egypt and Ethiopia founded the CAF, which has now grown to include more than 50 countries. The confederation runs tournaments for different age groups, including under-17 and under-21 competitions. At the top end, CAF organizes the African Champions League, won by Algeria's ES Sétif in 2014, and the popular and often exciting Africa Cup of Nations for national teams.

 ## UEFA

Full name: Union of European Football Associations
Headquarters: Nyon, Switzerland
Home to over 50 footballing nations of Europe, UEFA was formed in 1954. Its member nations have won the FIFA World Cup 11 times. UEFA organizes club competitions such as the Europa League and UEFA Champions League, as well as national competitions including the UEFA European Championship. A former leading goalscorer at the EUROs, Michel Platini, was UEFA's president from 2007 to 2015.

 ## CONCACAF

Full name: Confederation of North, Central America and Caribbean Association Football
Headquarters: Miami, USA
Founded in 1961, CONCACAF has 41 members including Central American teams such as Costa Rica and Honduras, Caribbean nations including Jamaica and Trinidad & Tobago, and the three big sides from North America: the USA, Mexico and Canada. It also includes two nations which lie on the South American continent – Suriname and Guyana.

 ## OFC

Full name: Oceania Football Confederation
Headquarters: Auckland, New Zealand
The smallest of all the confederations, the OFC consists of just 11 full members and three associate members (Kiribati, Niue and Tuvalu). It was formed in 1966 but only admitted as a FIFA confederation in 1996. Ten years later, its largest member, Australia, left to join the Asian Football Confederation.

PART 1: Club Football

Competition football began with the formation of clubs in 19th-century England. Sheffield FC are considered to be the oldest association football club still in existence. They were formed in 1857 and contested the first-ever derby game three years later, against new local rivals Hallam. Since then, thousands of football clubs have been formed all over the world, competing in everything from small, amateur competitions right up to the world's top leagues in Europe, South America and Asia.

The UEFA Champions League final is the pinnacle of club football. Real Madrid's 4-1 win over Atlético Madrid in 2014 set several records, including giving the Spanish club a record 10 titles. In 2017, at Cardiff's Millennium Stadium (above), Real Madrid triumphed over Juventus by the same scoreline, becoming the first team to defend the trophy since 1990 and taking their tally to 12 titles.

PREMIER LEAGUE

The English Football League began in 1888 and in 1992 the 22 teams in its top tier, Division One, broke away to form the English Premier League. More than 45 clubs have taken part in the now 20-team competition which, despite its name, has included two clubs from Wales – Swansea City and Cardiff City. With games broadcast to over 650 million homes all around the globe, the Premier League is the most-watched league in the world. Manchester United have dominated the competition, winning the title 13 times, but in 2013-14 they suffered their first Premier League finish outside the top three.

Leicester City celebrate their incredible 2015-16 season, with captain Wes Morgan holding the Premier League trophy aloft after their final home game of the season, a 3-1 win over Everton. Morgan was at the heart of a remarkably resilient defence that lost just three out of 38 matches to finish ten points clear of second-placed Arsenal.

PREMIER LEAGUE: Teams

THE INVINCIBLES

In 2003-04 Arsenal went the entire season unbeaten, winning 26 and drawing 12 games. The side was propelled by 30 goals from striker Thierry Henry (*left*) and bolstered at the back by German goalkeeper Jens Lehmann, the only player to feature in all 38 games. It was the first time a team had gone unbeaten in the English top division since Preston North End in 1888-89.

WINNERS AND LOSERS

In 2016-17, Chelsea broke the record for the most league wins in a 38-game season, with 30 victories. The previous record was 29, achieved by Chelsea in both 2004-05 and 2005-06. Derby County recorded the fewest wins in a season, when in 2007-08 they notched up just one victory, 1-0 over Newcastle. Their points tally of 11 was a record low for a Premier League season.

GOAL RECORDS

Chelsea's record 103 goals scored in 2009-10 was nearly equalled by Manchester City (102) in 2013-14, and the London club's record for conceding the fewest goals (15 in 2003-04) also remains intact. Swindon Town, in contrast, let in 100 goals in 1993-94, while Sunderland went on the longest Premier League losing run, defeated in 15 straight games in 2002-03.

TOP TEAMS

Just six teams have won the Premier League: Manchester City (*below*), Chelsea, Arsenal, Leicester City, Blackburn Rovers and Manchester United, whose tally of 89 points in 2011-12 was the most collected in a season without winning the league. Chelsea's 95 points when winning the 2004-05 title is the most gathered in a season.

MOST WINS AND POINTS IN THE PREMIER LEAGUE

Team	Wins	Points
Manchester United	604	2021
Arsenal	525	1822
Chelsea	516	1789
Liverpool	478	1677
Tottenham Hotspur	400	1447

Chelsea's players celebrate winning the Premier League title after defeating Crystal Palace 1-0 on 3 May 2015. Chelsea lost only three of their 38 league games all season.

PREMIER LEAGUE: Players

 SHEAR MAGIC

The most goals scored in the Premier League is 260 by Alan Shearer, who played for Blackburn Rovers between 1992 and 1996 before moving to Newcastle United for a then world-record fee of £15.6 million. Shearer also holds the record for the most Premier League hat-tricks – 11.

 RYAN'S RECORDS

No one has played in more Premier League games than Ryan Giggs, with 632 appearances for Manchester United. The Welsh winger, who became caretaker manager of United in 2013-14 and then assistant to manager Louis van Gaal, also has more Premier League championship medals (13) than any other player. He is also the only player to have scored in every one of the first 21 seasons of the Premier League.

MOST CAREER GOALS IN THE PREMIER LEAGUE

Player	Goals	Games
Alan Shearer	260	434
Wayne Rooney	198	460
Andrew Cole	189	408
Frank Lampard	177	609
Thierry Henry	175	258

US goalkeeper Brad Friedel holds the record for the most consecutive Premier League appearances. He played every single match between August 2004 and October 2012, a staggering 310 games.

GOAL FEATS

Tottenham Hotspur's Ledley King scored the Premier League's fastest goal, just 9.7 seconds after kick-off against Bradford City in 2000. Another Tottenham player, Jermain Defoe, scored five goals in a single half against Wigan Athletic in 2009. Spurs won 9-1, the second-biggest thrashing in Premier League history – just behind Manchester United's 9-0 defeat of Ipswich Town in 1995. In May 2015, Southampton's Sadio Mane scored the fastest Premier League hat-trick, in two minutes 56 seconds against Aston Villa.

BACK OF THE NET

Alan Shearer and Andrew Cole both scored 34 goals in a season when the Premier League featured 22 teams. The record for the current 20-team, 38-game format is 31 goals, jointly held by Alan Shearer, Cristiano Ronaldo and Luis Suárez. In the 2015-16 season, Leicester City's Jamie Vardy (*left*) set a Premier League record by scoring in 11 consecutive games.

PREMIER LEAGUE: Other records

REFS AND BOOKINGS

Michael Oliver (*above*) was 25 years and 182 days old when he took charge of Birmingham City v Blackburn Rovers in 2010 – the Premier League's youngest ever referee. The most yellow cards handed out to a team in a single Premier League match is nine, by referee Mark Clattenburg to Tottenham Hotspur during their May 2016 game versus Chelsea. The Premier League player with most yellow cards is midfielder Gareth Barry, who had incurred 119 bookings by the end of 2016-17.

MERRY-GO-ROUND

Two managers have coached five different clubs in the Premier League. Both Harry Redknapp (West Ham United, Southampton, Portsmouth, Tottenham Hotspur) and Mark Hughes (Blackburn Rovers, Manchester City, Fulham, Stoke City) also managed Queens Park Rangers in the 2012-13 season, with Redknapp replacing Hughes after he failed to win any of the team's first 12 games.

FIRST AND LAST

The very first Premier League goal was scored by Brian Deane for Sheffield United against Manchester United in August 1992. The latest goal scored in a Premier League game came in April 2011 between Arsenal and Liverpool. After treatment for Liverpool defender Jamie Carragher, the game went into a long period of added time, during which Dirk Kuyt scored a penalty (*right*) 12 minutes after full-time. The game ended 1-1.

PERFECT PERCENTAGE

Former Gunners defender Pat Rice won all three of his games as caretaker manager of Arsenal in 1996. Jim Barron of Aston Villa also has a perfect win ratio but was only in charge for one match. Among coaches in charge for more than ten games, Guus Hiddink's short spell at Chelsea in 2009 was the most successful, with 11 wins from 13 fixtures – a win ratio of 85 percent.

KING OF THE COACHES

No English manager has won the Premier League. The most successful manager, Sir Alex Ferguson (*left*), hailed from Scotland and coached Manchester United to all 13 of their Premier League titles in 21 seasons. Ferguson's record in the Premier League with Manchester United is: played 808 games, won 527 and lost only 114 – a win ratio of 65%.

BUNDESLIGA

The German Bundesliga began in 1963 with 16 teams. 1. FC Köln won the first competition and since then more than 50 clubs have taken part in what is now an 18-team league. Each season the bottom two teams are relegated, with their places taken by the top two sides from 2. Bundesliga. A third place in the top division is claimed by the winner of a two-game play-off between the team that finishes 16th and the third-placed team in 2. Bundesliga. With an average of over 43,000 fans at each match, the Bundesliga is the world's best-attended football league.

Borussia Dortmund have the largest football ground in Germany, holding over 80,000 devoted fans. The club was the first Bundesliga side to win a European title – the European Cup Winners' Cup in 1966.

BUNDESLIGA: Teams

 BRILLIANT BAYERN

No team has claimed the Bundesliga crown more times than Bayern Munich. The Bavarian club has won the title 26 times, most recently in 2016-17 – a staggering 21 titles more than the second most successful team. With their latest triumph, Bayern became the first side to win the Bundesliga five times in a row.

 TITLE DEFENDERS

Bayern Munich have not always had it their own way in the Bundesliga. They won the title for the first time in 1968-69, but it was the side that took their crown the following year, Borussia Mönchengladbach, who would go on to become the league's first record breakers. When *Die Fohlen* (The Foals) won the title again in 1970-71, they became the first team in Bundesliga history to make a successful defence of their title.

Bayern Munich were in irrepressible form in the 2013-14 season. They won a record 29 out of 34 matches, were crowned Bundesliga champions on 25 March (with a record seven games left to play) and finished the season with a points haul of 90 – a massive 19 points ahead of Borussia Dortmund in second.

⊚ ONE-TITLE WONDERS

Of the 12 teams to have won the title in the Bundesliga's 50-year history, four of them have claimed the championship on just one occasion: TSV 1860 München in 1965-66, Eintracht Braunschweig in 1966-67, 1. FC Nürnberg in 1967-68, and VfL Wolfsburg (*left*) in 2008-09.

MOST BUNDESLIGA TITLES

Team	Titles
Bayern Munich	26
Borussia Dortmund	5
Borussia Mönchengladbach	5
SV Werder Bremen	4
Hamburger SV	3
VfB Stuttgart	3

⊚ FROM PROMOTION TO CHAMPIONS

Just one team has been promoted from 2. Bundesliga to become top-division title-winners the following season: FC Kaiserslautern, who were crowned champions of Germany in 1997-98. It was a breakthrough season for legendary midfielder Michael Ballack (*left, in red*), who made his Bundesliga debut for the club against Karlsruher.

BUNDESLIGA: Players

THE BOMBER

When it comes to goalscoring in the Bundesliga, one player stands out – Gerd Müller, nicknamed *Der Bomber* (The Bomber). Blessed with quick acceleration and reactions, Müller scored twice on his debut for Bayern Munich in October 1964. The following season saw Müller and Bayern promoted from the Regionalliga Süd into the Bundesliga, where he went on to score an incredible 365 goals in 427 games. Müller was the Bundesliga's top scorer in seven seasons, but also holds an unwanted record for the most Bundesliga penalties missed – 12 out of 63 taken.

Coming on as a sub against VfL Wolfsburg in September 2015, Bayern's Robert Lewandowski scored five goals in just nine minutes. The Pole set a record for the quickest Bundesliga hat-trick in history, another for the fastest four-goal haul in one Bundesliga match, and yet another record with his fifth strike!

GOALSCORING GOALKEEPER

Hamburger SV goalkeeper Hans-Jörg Butt (*left, in yellow*) scored seven penalties in 1998-99 and a further nine the following season. After a move to Bayer Leverkusen in 2001, he scored at least one penalty in each of the next five seasons, ending up with a tally of 26 Bundesliga goals.

CHAMPION HAUL

Three players have won a record eight Bundesliga championships. Midfielders Mehmet Scholl and Bastian Schweinsteiger, plus legendary goalkeeper Oliver Kahn, won all their titles with Bayern Munich. Kahn also holds the Bundesliga record for the most clean sheets in a season (19 in 2001-02) and the most career clean sheets – 196 games.

 # CLEAN-SHEET CHAMPION

The quickest goalkeeper to record a century of clean sheets in the Bundesliga was Manuel Neuer, who reached the milestone in February 2017 during Bayern Munich's 8-0 victory over Hamburg. It was Neuer's 183rd game in the league.

 # MOST GAMES IN A ROW

Agile, brave and with lightning-fast reactions, goalkeeper Josef "Sepp" Maier played in a staggering 442 consecutive Bundesliga games for Bayern Munich from August 1966 to June 1979. Later that summer he was injured in a car crash which tragically ended his career.

MOST CAREER GOALS IN THE BUNDESLIGA

Player	Goals	Games
Gerd Müller	365	427
Klaus Fischer	268	535
Jupp Heynckes	220	369
Manfred Burgsmüller	213	447
Ulf Kirsten	182	350

BUNDESLIGA: Other records

 ## UNBELIEVABLE UDO

Udo Lattek was a coaching assistant to the West German team that reached the 1966 FIFA World Cup final, and he went on to become the most successful Bundesliga coach ever. He won eight league titles: three with Bayern Munich (1971-72, 1972-73, 1973-74), followed by two for Borussia Mönchengladbach (1975-76, 1976-77) and another three in a row, again with Bayern (1984-85, 1985-86, 1986-87).

 ## YOUNGEST AND OLDEST

Matthias Sammer (*near left*) won three Bundesliga titles as a player, with VfB Stuttgart (1991-92) and Borussia Dortmund (1994-95, 1995-96). In 2000, he was appointed head coach of Borussia Dortmund where, in 2002 at the age of 34 years, 241 days, he became the youngest ever Bundesliga-winning coach. In contrast, Jupp Heynckes (*far left*) became the oldest winning coach (68 years, 9 days) when he steered Bayern Munich to the 2012-13 title.

GOALS, GOALS, GOALS

The most goals scored in a season was 1,097 in the 306 matches of the 1983-84 competition – an average of 3.58 goals per game. The same season saw the most goals scored on a single matchday – 53. On five occasions, 12 goals have been scored in a single game but only one team, Borussia Mönchengladbach, netted a dozen times, thrashing Borussia Dortmund in 1978.

Otto Rehhagel managing Berlin's Hertha BSC in 2012, the team he made his Bundesliga debut for as a defender back in 1963.

LONG SERVICE

Werder Bremen certainly believe in continuity. Two of their coaches top the table for the most seasons at one club. Otto Rehhagel spent 15 years in charge (1976, 1981-95), with Thomas Schaaf just behind him on 14 seasons as coach (1999-2013). Rehhagel has spent an incredible 29 seasons in the Bundesliga as a coach, taking charge of eight clubs including Kickers Offenbach, Borussia Dortmund and, in 2012, Hertha BSC.

HIGHEST AND LOWEST

The largest official Bundesliga attendance occurred in 1969, when 88,075 fans watched Hertha BSC play 1. FC Köln. The lowest attendance (827) happened during SC Tasmania 1900 Berlin's disastrous 1965-66 season, when they won only two games and were relegated with a record low of eight points.

LA LIGA

The Primera División, or La Liga, kicked off for the first time in 1929 with just ten teams. It now contains 20 Spanish sides competing in what UEFA have rated in recent years as the strongest league in the world. For a decade (1963-73) many foreign footballers were banned from playing in La Liga, but today it is home to global superstars including Argentina's Lionel Messi, Portugal's Cristiano Ronaldo and Welsh international Gareth Bale. Although nine different clubs have won La Liga, the competition is dominated by the two giants Barcelona and Real Madrid, who have won 57 league titles between them.

Barcelona's Luis Suárez holds off Real Madrid, who won their last ten league games of 2015-16 but fell short of champions Barça by one point. Suárez became the first player to score four goals in back-to-back La Liga games on his way to topping the scoring chart with 40 goals.

LA LIGA: Teams

REAL ON A RUN

Real Madrid (*below*) have won La Liga 33 times, nine times more than fierce rivals Barcelona. Their league championship success includes two periods during which they won La Liga five times in a row (1961-65 and 1986-90), the only team to have done so. Real also hold the records for most La Liga wins (1,647), most goals in a season (121 in 2011-12) and the most goals scored in total – a staggering 5,946.

GOAL GLUTS

The biggest thrashing in La Liga history occurred in 1931, when Athletic Bilbao beat Barcelona 12-1. Bilbao scored only three goals fewer that day than Club Deportivo Logroñés managed in a whole La Liga season (15 in 1994-95). Bilbao were also involved in the highest-scoring draw, a 6-6 thriller against Atlético Madrid in 1950, and in the game with the most goals, a 9-5 win over Racing de Santander in 1933.

GETTING IN ON THE ACT

While Barcelona and Real Madrid have dominated many seasons, they have not had things all their own way. Athletic Bilbao, Villareal and Real Sociedad have all been La Liga runners-up in the past 16 years, while Atlético Madrid, Valencia (*right*, champions in 2004) and Deportivo la Coruña have all snatched titles since 1995.

 # BRILLIANT BARÇA

Barcelona have finished in the top three of La Liga 61 times, including an agonising 25 runners-up finishes, more than any other team. In recent seasons, the Camp Nou stadium has proved to be an intimidating fortress. In 2009-10 and 2012-13, Barça managed to score 55 out of a possible 57 points at home. The only blots on a perfect home record were a 1-1 draw with Villareal (2009-10) and a 2-2 tie with Real Madrid (2012-13). In both seasons, Barça were crowned champions.

MOST LA LIGA TITLES

Team	Titles
Real Madrid	33
Barcelona	24
Atlético Madrid	10
Athletic Bilbao	8
Valencia	6
Real Sociedad	2
Deportivo la Coruña	1
Sevilla	1
Real Betis	1

Coach Diego Simeone is thrown into the air by his delighted Atlético Madrid players after a draw against Barcelona saw them win La Liga in 2013-14, 18 years since their last title.

HAT-TRICK HEROES

Real Madrid's Cristiano Ronaldo and Barcelona's Lionel Messi trade La Liga records year in, year out. Both top the charts for the number of hat-tricks scored in La Liga. Messi has 26 but, after scoring two hat-tricks in 2016-17, Ronaldo leads with 32.

Cristiano Ronaldo's £80-million move to Real Madrid in 2009 made him the most expensive footballer in history at the time.

MAGICAL MESSI

His team may not have collected the league title that year, but five-time FIFA Ballon d'Or winner Lionel Messi was in sparkling form during the 2011-12 season. The Barcelona forward scored a staggering 50 goals in 37 appearances – an all-time La Liga record for one season.

THE MEDAL COLLECTOR

Superfast with or without the ball, and tremendously skilful as well, Francisco Gento signed for Real Madrid in 1952-53 aged 19. A key player in the side during the club's golden years, he collected 12 league championship winners' medals – more than any other player in La Liga history.

GOALS GALORE

Cristiano Ronaldo has set La Liga on fire since he joined Real Madrid from Manchester United in 2009. The multi-talented Portuguese forward has scored 285 goals in 265 games – La Liga's all-time record scoring rate.

RECORD KEEPER

Goalkeeper Andoni Zubizarreta enjoyed an eye-catching career with Athletic Bilbao, Barcelona, Valencia and Spain. He played at four FIFA World Cups, three UEFA European Championships, won a then-record 126 caps for his country and claimed two league championships with Athletic Bilbao in 1982-83 and 1983-84. He played a staggering 622 La Liga matches – an all-time record.

MOST CAREER GOALS IN LA LIGA

Player	Goals	Games
Lionel Messi	349	382
Cristiano Ronaldo	285	265
Telmo Zarra	251	279
Hugo Sanchez	234	347
Raúl	228	550

LA LIGA: Other records

 ## MAGNIFICENT MIGUEL

Of Real Madrid's 38 full-time managers, Miguel Muñoz (*left, with the ball*) had the longest and most successful spell in charge. The former midfielder made over 230 La Liga appearances as a player for Real, winning four league championships and three European Cups. He then coached the team from 1960 to 1974, winning a record nine La Liga titles and two European Cups.

 ## KING CRUYFF AND PRINCE PEP

Barcelona's most successful manager is the former Dutch attacking maestro Johan Cruyff, who won four La Liga titles in a row and one European Cup between 1988 and 1996. Playing in Cruyff's team was defensive midfielder Josep "Pep" Guardiola (*right*). He went on to become Barça's second most successful manager, with three La Liga championships and two UEFA Champions League titles.

MOST LA LIGA GAMES COACHED

Manager	Games	Years
Luis Aragonés	757	1974-2004
Javier Irureta	614	1988-2008
Miguel Muñoz	608	1958-82
Víctor Fernández	535	1990-2015
Javier Clemente	512	1981-2012

SHORT-TERM SUPREMOS

In contrast to Miguel Muñoz's long reign, Vicente del Bosque had three spells as coach of Real Madrid. The shortest lasted for just a single game in January 1996 after the previous coach, Jorge Valdano, had resigned. One Real manager, José Antonio Camacho, took charge in the summer of 1998, but left after only 22 days and no games in charge.

RED-CARD RECORDS

The most red cards in a single La Liga game occurred during an Espanyol-Barcelona match in 2003. The referee, Alfonso Zamorano, sent off six players, three from each side. Eleven years later, Real Madrid's Sergio Ramos received his 19th La Liga red card with a foul on Barcelona's Neymar (*left*). In April 2017, Ramos extended his unwanted league record to 22 red cards, the last coming with a foul on another Barça player, Lionel Messi.

SERIE A

Formed in 1929, Italy's Serie A has attracted the cream of the world's footballers. More Serie A teams have reached the final of the UEFA Champions League/ European Cup than clubs from any other country. Since 2004, 20 teams – including globally famous sides such as Juventus and AC Milan – have competed alongside less well-known clubs such as Frosinone Calcio, who made their Serie A debut in the 2015-16 season after gaining promotion from Serie B. The Serie A title is also known as the *Scudetto*, after the small shield that the champions wear on their football strips the following season.

The Stadio Giuseppe Meazza, also known as the San Siro, is packed with 73,855 fans at the AC Milan-Inter Milan derby in May 2014. The ground hosted 2016-17's biggest attendance, with 78,328 fans seeing Inter draw 2-2 with AC Milan.

SERIE A: Teams

 ## THE OLD LADY SINGS

Founded in 1897, Juventus are the oldest and most successful Serie A club with 31 titles. In 2017, they recorded their sixth title in a row to set another Serie A record. In 2011-12, the team nicknamed The Old Lady or The Zebras (for their black-and-white striped shirts), went unbeaten for all 38 games of the season, letting in only 20 goals on the way to the title.

Juventus players celebrate a magnificent 2015-16 season in which they won their fifth Serie A title in a row. Their 2013-14 points tally of 102 remains a Serie A record.

STADIUM STABLEMATES

Inter Milan share the San Siro with their fierce rivals AC Milan, known as the *Rossoneri* (Red and Blacks). AC Milan played Torino in December 1993 at the San Siro in front of Serie A's largest official crowd – 85,848. The Rossoneri won that game 1-0, but in other seasons the stadium has seen AC Milan involved in the most goal-filled games: a 9-3 win over Atalanta in 1973 and three 11-goal thrillers (5-6 v Inter in 1949, and 9-2 v Novara Calcio and 4-7 v Atalanta in 1950).

INTER'S RUN

Including 2017-18, Inter Milan have spent 86 seasons in Serie A – more than any other club. They have won 16 league championships, including five Scudettos in a row between 2005-06 and 2009-10. In 2006-07, Inter won 30 matches, including a record 17-game winning streak, and notched up 94 points, a Serie A record at the time.

TRIUMPH AND TRAGEDY

Torino were once the best side in Serie A, winning five titles in the 1940s. In the 1947-48 season, they recorded the league's biggest scoreline, a 10-0 mauling of US Alessandria Calcio 1912. The following year, a plane crash claimed the lives of the entire team. Since then, Torino have won the Scudetto only once, in 1975-76.

MOST SERIE A TITLES

Team	Titles
Juventus	31
Inter Milan	16
AC Milan	15
Torino	6
Bologna	5

HOME ADVANTAGE

In September 2015, Juventus began a record-breaking run of 33 Serie A victories at home, a sequence which was only broken in May 2017 when they drew 1-1 with Torino.

SERIE A: Players

 ## GOLDEN-BOOT GUNNAR

In the last decade, only two players have won the *Capocannoniere* (Golden Boot) for being Serie A's top scorer in two seasons: Zlatan Ibrahimović (2008-09 with Inter Milan and 2011-12 with AC Milan) and Antonio di Natale (2009-10 and 2010-11 with Udinese). AC Milan's Swedish striker Gunnar Nordahl was a scoring sensation in the 1950s, winning five Golden Boots in six seasons.

 ## GOALS IN A SEASON

The most Serie A goals in a season is 36, scored by Gino Rossetti in the 1928-29 season. In the 2015-16 season, Gonzalo Higuain tied the record whilst playing for Napoli.

 ## LEFT BACK LEGEND

Paolo Maldini (*far right*) made his Serie A debut in the 1984-85 season and did not retire until 2009. A fast, skilful and tenacious tackler, he played a staggering 647 Serie A games, all for AC Milan either at left back or in the centre of defence. Amazingly, Maldini was only the eighth-oldest player in Serie A, behind his defensive team-mate Alessandro Costacurta and the oldest player of all – Lazio keeper Marco Ballotta, who was 44 years and 38 days old when he played his last Serie A game in 2008.

Francesco Totti joined AS Roma in 1989, aged just 13, and played for the club until the end of the 2016-17 season, notching up an incredible 786 appearances in all competitions. He is the second-highest Serie A goalscorer of all time, with 250 goals.

TOP GOALIE

Gianluigi Buffon became Serie A's (and the world's) most expensive goalkeeper in 2001 when he was transferred from Parma to Juventus for a fee of £32.6 million. He has won eight Serie A championships with Juventus and a record 11 Serie A Goalkeeper of the Year awards. His tally of 168 caps for Italy, with whom he won the 2006 FIFA World Cup, make him the national record holder.

MOST CAREER GOALS IN SERIE A

Player	Goals	Games
Silvio Piola	274	537
Francesco Totti	250	619
Gunnar Nordahl	225	291
Giuseppe Meazza	216	367
José Altafini	216	459

SERIE A: Other records

 TERRIFIC TRAPATTONI

Giovanni Trapattoni has won ten league titles in four different countries: Italy, Germany, Portugal and Austria. His successes include a record seven Serie A titles: six with Juventus and one with Inter Milan. Trapattoni also coached AC Milan, Cagliari, Fiorentina and, outside of Italy, Bayern Munich, Benfica and Red Bull Salzburg.

 FIVE ALIVE

Marcello Lippi and Fabio Capello are the joint-second most successful Serie A coaches, both with five titles. One of Capello's former clubs, Roma, conceded a goal in May 2017 to Genoa's Pietro Pelligri who at 16 years, 2 months and 11 days, is Serie A's youngest ever goalscorer.

 MANAGER MERRY-GO-ROUND

Alberto Malesani has managed more Serie A teams than any other coach – 11, including Fiorentina, Parma, Verona, Modena, Udinese, Empoli, Siena, Bologna, Genoa and Palermo. In January 2014 he was appointed coach of US Sassuolo in their first season in Serie A. Malesani has actually had 12 coaching stints in Serie A. In the 2011-12 season, he was sacked as Genoa coach in December, then re-hired the following April only to be sacked again 20 days later!

YOUNG UDINESE

The youngest team to line up in the 2013-14 Serie A season was the Udinese side that played at Fiorentina in April. With the exception of two veteran central defenders, the team were all 23 years old or under, with goalkeeper Simone Scuffet (*left*) just 17. Udinese's manager at the time, Francesco Guidolin, has coached more Serie A games than anyone else – more than 550 in 17 seasons at six different Italian clubs.

AC Milan's Gabriel Paletta (left) is sent off against Bologna in February 2017. Milan were down to nine men by the 59th minute, but pulled off an astonishing 1-0 win with a goal from Mario Pasalic with just one minute of normal time remaining.

RED RAGE

AC Milan defender Gabriel Paletta received a joint record five red cards in the 2016-17 Serie A season, taking his total to nine, the most of any player in the league and one ahead of Felipe Melo. Midfielder Daniele Conti has been sent off only once, but holds the record for the most yellow cards in Serie A, a total of 99.

LIGUE 1

The top league in France began in 1932 with 20 teams, the number that still compete today. Ligue 1 has seen fantastic homegrown players such as Michel Platini and Zinedine Zidane, plus some outstanding foreign stars including Zlatan Ibrahimović and Thiago Silva. Over 75 clubs have played in the league, 14 of them – including US Boulogne, Gazélec Ajaccio and Dijon – for just one season. Ligue 1 stadiums tend to be smaller than in other major leagues. Of the 2016-17 clubs, only Lille, Marseille and Lyon boast stadiums capable of holding more than 50,000 fans. It was the club with the 16th biggest stadium in Ligue 1, Monaco, which scooped the title that season.

The Monaco team celebrate with the 2016-17 Ligue 1 championship trophy after finishing eight points clear of Paris Saint-Germain. Monaco won 30 of their 38 games – a record shared with PSG (2015-16) – and scored 107 goals, the most since RC Paris in the 1959-60 season.

LIGUE 1: Teams

 ## SUPER SAINT-ÉTIENNE

Nineteen clubs have won Ligue 1 since Olympique Lillois became the first in 1932-33. The last club to win it for the first time was Montpellier HSC in the 2011-12 season. AS Saint-Étienne have triumphed a record ten times, the last in 1980-81. They are followed by Olympique de Marseille (*below*) with nine titles, and Monaco and FC Nantes with eight.

 ## LIONS OF SOCHAUX

No team has spent more seasons in Ligue 1 than Sochaux. *Les Lionceaux* (The Lion Cubs) have won the championship twice, in 1934-35 and 1937-38. They hold the record for the most draws in Ligue 1 (632) and most losses (877), but not the most wins. That record is held by Marseille, who recorded their 1,056th win in Ligue 1 on 20 May 2017 – a 1-0 victory over Bastia.

MOST LIGUE 1 TITLES

Team	Titles
AS Saint-Étienne	10
Olympique de Marseille	9
FC Nantes	8
AS Monaco	8
Olympique Lyonnais	7
Stade de Reims	6
Bordeaux	6
Paris Saint-Germain	6

RECORD RUN

No club had won more than four Ligue 1 championships in a row until Olympique Lyonnais (Lyon for short), began to dominate French football in the 2000s. Propelled by attacking talents including Sidney Govou and Karim Benzema, and powerhouse midfielders such as Michael Essien, Lyon swept all before them, winning the first of seven consecutive Ligue 1 titles in 2001-02.

Marco Verratti crosses the ball during PSG's record-breaking 5-0 win over FC Nantes in January 2014. PSG completed the highest number of passes in a Ligue 1 match (863) and their players made a record 1,048 touches of the ball during the game.

POWERFUL PSG

With star players including Edinson Cavani, Zlatan Ibrahimović and the league's leading assists-maker, Ángel di Maria, Paris Saint-Germain were rampant in the 2015-16 season. They scored 102 goals, conceded just 19 and finished a staggering 31 points clear of Lyon, on 96 points – an all-time Ligue 1 record.

LIGUE 1: Players

 MEDAL HAUL

Five players have won seven Ligue 1 titles. Midfielder Jean-Michel Larqué and striker Hervé Revelli won theirs with AS Saint-Étienne (1966-67 to 1969-70 and 1973-74 to 1975-76) while goalkeeper Grégory Coupet and attacking midfielders Sidney Govou and Juninho Pernambucano collected theirs as part of Olympique Lyonnais' incredible seven consecutive titles (2001-02 to 2007-08).

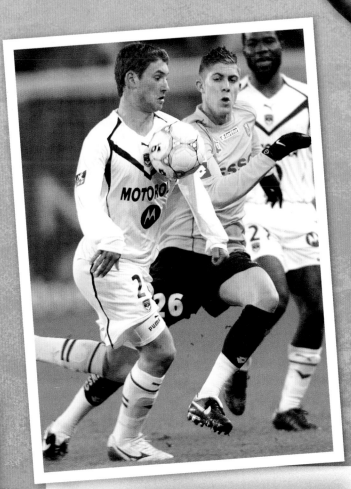

 DEADLY DELIO

An Argentinian who was nicknamed The Italian, Delio Onnis spent most of his career in the French league, playing for four clubs from 1971 to 1986: Stade de Reims, AS Monaco, Tours FC and Sporting Toulon Var. Onnis was a predatory striker, and Ligue 1's leading scorer in five seasons. He rarely wore shinpads and struck 299 times, making him Ligue 1's all-time top scorer. In second place, 44 goals behind, is the Bordeaux and Lyon striker Bernard Lacombe.

 YOUNG GUNS

Laurent Paganelli became the youngest ever player in Ligue 1 when he came on for AS Saint-Étienne as a half-time substitute in 1978. Paganelli was just 15 years, 10 months old at the time. In 2005 against Bordeaux, Sochaux's winger Jérémy Ménez (*above, in yellow*) became the youngest to score a hat-trick. He was 17 years, 260 days old.

Zlatan Ibrahimović, PSG's all-time leading goalscorer, finished the 2015-16 season as the league's top scorer, with 38 goals in just 31 games. He also scored Ligue 1's quickest ever hat-trick in March 2016, in just nine minutes against Troyes AC.

BIG BUYS

Star strikers and attackers always attract the highest transfer fees. The world's first £10-million player was Jean-Pierre Papin, who moved from Olympique de Marseille to AC Milan in 1992. On 31 May 2013, AS Monaco broke the Ligue 1 transfer record by paying 60 million Euros for Colombian striker Radamel Falcao. The record lasted just over a month, when rivals Paris Saint-Germain spent 64.5 million Euros to buy Uruguayan goalscorer Edinson Cavani.

MOST GAMES PLAYED IN LIGUE 1

Player	Games	Years
Mickaël Landreau	618	1997-2014
Jean-Luc Ettori	602	1975-94
Dominique Dropsy	596	1972-89
Dominique Baratelli	593	1967-85
Alain Giresse	586	1970-88

SUPER STOPPER

During the 2004-05 and 2005-06 seasons, AS Saint-Étienne goalkeeper Jérémie Janot kept 17 consecutive clean sheets at home – 1,534 minutes without letting in a goal. In 2012, the veteran goalkeeper moved to Le Mans after 16 seasons at Saint-Étienne.

LIGUE 1: Other records

CHAMPION COACHES

Albert Batteux is the most successful Ligue 1 coach, with five titles at Stade de Reims (1953, 1955, 1958, 1960, 1962) and three with AS Saint-Étienne (1968, 1969, 1970). Robert Herbin coached Saint-Étienne to four championships in 1974, 1975, 1976 and 1981, while Laurent Blanc has won three titles with Paris Saint-Germain (2014 to 2016) as well as the 2008-09 title as coach of Bordeaux.

WHAT A GUY!

In 1961, Guy Roux became manager of AJ Auxerre aged just 22. He went on to coach the small-town club for a record 890 matches in Ligue 1, astonishingly winning the title in 1995-96. French legends Eric Cantona, Laurent Blanc and Djibril Cissé were all coached by Roux during his long time in charge (1961-2000 and 2001-05).

REPEAT FEATS

Jean-Pierre Papin is the only player to be Ligue 1's leading goalscorer for five seasons in a row, from 1987-88. André Abegglen (playing for Sochaux in 1935) and Jean Nicolas (for Rouen in 1938) jointly hold the record for most goals scored in a single game – seven.

RAPID RED

The fastest sending off in Ligue 1 occurred in February 2013 during a match between Olympique de Marseille and Evian. Marseille striker Jordan Ayew (*right*) came on as a substitute and left the pitch one minute, 51 seconds later after receiving two yellow cards from referee Antony Gautier for bad fouls.

MOST GOALS IN A LIGUE 1 SEASON

Player (club)	Goals	Season
Josip Skoblar (Marseille)	44	1970-71
Zlatan Ibrahimović (PSG)	38	2015-16
Carlos Bianchi (Stade de Reims, PSG)	37	1977-78
Philippe Gondet (FC Nantes)	36	1965-66
Edinson Cavani (PSG)	35	2016-17
Serge Masnaghetti (Valenciennes)	35	1962-63
Gunnar Andersson (Marseille)	35	1952-53

Lyon's players celebrate with the Ligue 1 trophy in 2007 after becoming the first team in any of the big five leagues in Europe to win six titles in a row.

TOP COACHES

After scooping the 2015 and 2016 titles, Laurent Blanc is the only three-time winner of the official Ligue 1 coach award, his first coming in 2008 with Bordeaux. His predecessor at PSG, Carlo Ancelotti, was the joint winner of the 2013 award and was transferred that year to Real Madrid for a fee believed to be 3.8 million Euros, the most paid for a Ligue 1 coach.

EUROPEAN CLUB FOOTBALL

Europe is the engine room of world club football. The majority of the planet's wealthiest, most successful teams are found there and they attract the very best professional footballers from all over the globe.

In 2013 Gibraltar became the 54th member of UEFA (Union of European Football Associations), the body responsible for organizing football in Europe. Its eight-team league is one of the continent's smallest. Austria and Switzerland's top flights both contain ten teams, Slovakia and Kosovo (which joined UEFA in May 2016 to become the 55th and newest member) have 12 teams and Denmark has 14. Sweden, Russia, Poland and Greece run 16-team leagues, while Romania has 18.

Spartak Moscow (*in red*) clash with CSKA Moscow in the Russian Premier League. Spartak have won the league a record ten times, most recently in 2016-17. CSKA are second in the table, with six titles including back-to-back wins in 2012-13 and 2013-14.

EUROPEAN CLUB FOOTBALL: Teams

 DOMESTIC DOMINANCE

In 1891 Glasgow Rangers and Dumbarton FC shared the first ever Scottish league title. Rangers have gone on to win 53 more titles – the most league championships of any European club. Rangers have won more than 44% of all the Scottish titles available. Only the Greek side Olympiacos (*left, in red and white*), have dominated more in Europe, winning 44 of 81 league titles (54.3%).

 PREMIUM PRIMEIRA

The Portuguese Primeira Liga has seen many outstanding teams, including Sporting Clube de Portugal, with 18 league titles, and Porto with 27 championships to their name. The most successful of all has been Benfica with 36 league titles, including the 2016-17 championship. In 1972-73, Benfica became the first Portuguese side to go unbeaten through a season, winning 28 and drawing two of their 30 matches. They repeated the feat in 1977-78, but nine draws meant that they ended as runners-up to Porto.

MOST CONSECUTIVE LEAGUE WINS

Team	Wins	Seasons
Benfica (Portugal)	29	1971-72 to 1972-73
Dinamo Zagreb (Croatia)	28	2006-07 to 2007-08
The New Saints (Wales)	27	2016-17
Celtic (Scotland)	25	2003-04
Dinamo Tirana (Albania)	25	1951–52
Red Star Belgrade (Serbia)	24	2015-16
Shakhtar Donetsk (Ukraine)	24	2011-12 to 2012-13

⚽ BOLD AND BOLDER

Kjøbenhavns Boldklub was one of the oldest football clubs in continental Europe, founded in the 1870s and winning 15 Danish league titles (the last in 1980). In 1992 KB merged with Copenhagen neighbours Boldklubben 1903 (themselves seven-times league winners) to form FC Copenhagen (*right*), who won the 1992-93 title at their first attempt.

Luuk de Jong (*left*) topped the Eredivisie goal chart in 2014-15 as PSV won their 22nd Dutch title. De Jong's 26 goals in 2015-16 helped secure back-to-back titles for PSV, who lie second in the table of Dutch league champions, ten wins behind Ajax (33 victories).

⚽ UNBEATEN RUN

In the last game of the 1985-86 season, FC Steaua Bucharest beat Universitatea Craiova in a 5-4 thriller. It started an incredible unbeaten run in the Romanian league that lasted 104 games and spanned three full seasons – including an 11-0 thrashing of Corvinul Hunedoara. The run ended in the third game of the 1989-90 season, with defeat to Dinamo Bucharest.

EUROPEAN CLUB FOOTBALL: Leagues

FIVE STARS

Only five clubs have won the Turkish Süper Lig. Galatasaray top the winners' table with 20 titles, followed by Fenerbahçe (19), Beşiktaş (15), Trabzonspor (6) and the newest winners, Bursaspor. The latter triumphed in 2009-10 after beating defending champions Beşiktaş 2-1 in the final game of the season.

HARD TO BEAT

Away from home, Dynamo Kiev proved impossible to beat in the Ukrainian Premier League for 51 games in a row – a run that started in the 2005-06 season. The next-best run away from home in Europe is held by Galatasaray, who between 1998 and 2000 went unbeaten on the road for 40 matches.

CONSECUTIVE KINGS

The European record for most league titles in a row is 14, shared by Skonto FC – who were champions of the Latvian Higher League every season from 1991 to 2004 – and Lincoln Red Imps, the champions of Gibraltar from 2003 to 2016.

⚽ TREMENDOUS TWENTE

Fifteen teams have won the Dutch Eredivisie just once. The most recent was in 2009-10, when FC Twente, managed by Steve McLaren (*right*) and propelled by 24 league goals from Bryan Ruiz, won 16 of their 17 home games to pip Ajax by one point.

MOST POINTS IN A EUROPEAN LEAGUE

Team	Points	Season
Celtic	106	2016-17
Celtic	103	2001-02
Juventus	102	2013-14
Real Madrid	100	2011-12
Barcelona	100	2012-13
Barcelona	99	2009-10
Celtic	99	2013-14

Galatasaray's Felipe Melo (*right*) competes for the ball in a Turkish Süper Lig clash against arch-rivals and 2013-14 champions, Fenerbahçe.

⚽ UP AND DOWN

In highly competitive leagues with promotion and relegation, teams can frequently bounce in and out of the top flight. KV Mechelen have been promoted to or relegated from the Belgian Pro League 23 times. Aris Limassol have moved between the top and second division in Cyprus a record 28 times, 17 of which came in a 19-season period between 1996-97 and 2014-15.

EUROPEAN CLUB FOOTBALL: Players

GREAT GOALSCORERS

Ferenc Déak dazzled in the Hungarian league in 1945-46, scoring an astonishing 66 league goals for Szentlórinci in just 34 games. Coen Dillen's 43 goals for PSV Eindhoven in 1957 is the most scored by one player in a Dutch league season. Another PSV player, Willy van der Kuijlen (*right*), holds the record for the most career goals in the Dutch league with an incredible 311. He is matched by the Turkish league record-holder Metin Oktay of Galatasaray.

GOLDEN SHOE WINNERS

The European Golden Shoe is awarded to the highest goalscorer in a league season. Cristiano Ronaldo (2007-08, 2010-11, 2013-14 and 2014-15) and Lionel Messi (2009-10, 2011-12, 2012-13 and 2016-17) top the table with four wins each. Messi's 50 goals in 2011-12 is a record for the most scored in a league season. Five of the nine players who have won the Golden Shoe twice, including Eusébio and Ally McCoist, did so playing in leagues outside the Big Five (England, Spain, Italy, Germany and France).

BRILLIANT BICAN

The ultimate goal machine in European club football is Josef Bican. The Czech-Austrian was as quick as many 100-metre sprinters of his era and could shoot powerfully with both feet. He played for several clubs but is most remembered for his time with Slavia Prague (1937-48), where he scored an incredible 534 goals in 274 games. In total, football historians estimate he scored over 800 goals in competitive European club matches.

⚽ DEFIANT DANY

Belgian goalkeeper Dany Verlinden holds the European record for the most time in goal in league games without conceding. Playing for Belgian side Club Brugge, the keeper saw a staggering 1,390 minutes of action between March and September 1990 without once picking the ball out of the back of his net.

Sporting Clube de Portugal's Mário Jardel celebrates scoring one of his staggering tally of 42 goals in 30 Primeira Liga games in the 2001-02 season.

⚽ HAT-TRICK HEROES

Brazilians have scored 75 hat-tricks in the Portuguese Primeira Liga, with Mário Jardel striking 13 of them. The fastest-known hat-trick in a European league was scored by Tommy Ross for Ross County in the Northern Ireland league in 1964. Ross, an 18-year-old defender, struck three goals in just 90 seconds. In two months in 2017, Dutchman Bas Doost scored four hat-tricks for Sporting Lisbon.

EUROPEAN CLUB FOOTBALL: Other records

FIRST LADIES

In 2003, Nicole Petignat (*left*) became the first female referee of a men's match in a UEFA competition. She took charge of a UEFA Cup game between Swedish club AIK Fotboll and Fylkir from Iceland. Eleven years later, Corinne Diacre became the most senior female coach in men's European football when she was appointed head coach of the French Ligue 2 club Clermont Foot.

TERRIFIC TOMISLAV

Croatian Tomislav Ivić was the first coach to win league titles in five European nations: the former Yugoslavia with Hajduk Split (1974, 1975, 1979), the Netherlands with Ajax (1977), Belgium with Anderlecht (1981), Greece with Panathinaikos (1986) and Portugal with Porto (1988).

MEGA COACHES

With 49 trophies won (10 at Aberdeen and 39 at Manchester United), Sir Alex Ferguson is the most successful manager in Europe. He is tied with Giovanni Trappatoni on seven UEFA competition trophies while his tally of 16 league titles places him three ahead of the Ukrainian coach Valeriy Lobanovskyi, who took Dynamo Kiev to 13 league titles, nine cups and two European Cup Winners' Cup triumphs.

RECORD CROWDS

The biggest recorded attendance for a UEFA competition match was at Hampden Park in Glasgow, Scotland in 1970, when a record 136,505 people watched Celtic beat Leeds United 2-1. In 1987, 135,000 supporters crammed into Portugal's original Estádio da Luz (*right*) to watch Benfica play arch-rivals Porto.

MAGICAL MOURINHO

Portuguese coach Jose Mourinho made a major impact in his first decade in football management. The first four teams he coached – Porto, Chelsea, Inter Milan and Real Madrid – put together a total unbeaten run at home of 150 league games over nine years. Between 2002 and 2011 Mourinho's teams scored 342 goals, conceded 87 and won 125 times.

OLDEST CUP

The oldest existing cup competition in Europe is the English FA Cup, which was first held in 1871-72. Arsenal lead the way with 13 victories, most recently in 2017, followed by Manchester United with 12 and Tottenham Hotspur with eight. Chelsea, Aston Villa and Liverpool have won the competition seven times.

Arsenal manager Arsène Wenger celebrates with the FA Cup in 2017 after a 2-1 win over Chelsea. Aaron Ramsey's winning goal moved Arsenal to the top of the all-time winners table and made Wenger the most successful manager in FA Cup history, with seven wins.

UEFA CHAMPIONS LEAGUE

A championship to find the best club side in Europe began in 1955. The European Cup originally featured only the winners of various national leagues. Each team played an opponent in two games, home and away, in each round leading up to a single-game final. For the 1992-93 season, the European Cup received a makeover. There was a new name – the UEFA Champions League – and a change in format, with teams competing in mini-leagues, known as groups, with knockout rounds at the later stages. The UEFA Champions League is now the biggest, most glamorous club competition in world football.

Real Madrid celebrate *La Decima* – their tenth UEFA Champions League or European Cup triumph in 2014. Real are the undisputed kings of the competition, winning a record 12th title in 2017 to move five titles clear of AC Milan in the list of all-time winners.

UEFA CHAMPIONS LEAGUE: Teams

 DOMINANT ALL WHITES

Real Madrid (*below*) dominated the early seasons of the European Cup, winning the first five competitions, including an epic 7-3 victory over Eintracht Frankfurt in the 1960 final. The Spanish giants have won the competition 12 times and have appeared in the semi-finals on a record 28 occasions, including the last seven seasons (2011-17).

 MOST GOALS IN A MATCH

Dutch side Feyenoord beat Iceland's KR Reykjavik 12-2 in the first round of the 1969-70 European Cup. Over two legs, the biggest-ever aggregate score was by Portugal's Benfica, who beat Stade Dudelange of Luxembourg 8-0 away and 10-0 at home in 1965.

FINAL FINISH

Six teams have a perfect record in the final. Four won the only final they reached: Feyenoord (1970), Aston Villa (1982), PSV Eindhoven (1988) and Red Star Belgrade (1991). Two clubs have won both finals they have contested: Nottingham Forest (1979, 1980) and Porto (1987 and 2004, shown right).

TOSS OF A COIN

In the past, ways to decide a drawn knockout match included the toss of a coin. This was last used in the 1969-70 European Cup after Celtic and Benfica drew 3-3. Celtic won the toss and went on to beat Fiorentina and Leeds United to reach the final.

Barcelona's Brazilian attacker Neymar scored the last goal of the 2014-15 final, in a 3-1 victory over Juventus. He finished the campaign as joint top scorer with ten goals alongside teammate Lionel Messi and Real Madrid's Cristiano Ronaldo.

MOST EUROPEAN CUP/ CHAMPIONS LEAGUE TROPHIES

Team	Wins	Years
Real Madrid	12	1956-60, 1966, 1998, 2000, 2002, 2014, 2016, 2017
AC Milan	7	1963, 1969, 1989, 1990, 1994, 2003, 2007
Bayern Munich	5	1974, 1975, 1976, 2001, 2013
Liverpool	5	1977, 1978, 1981, 1984, 2005
Barcelona	5	1992, 2006, 2009, 2011, 2015
Ajax	4	1971, 1972, 1973, 1995

UEFA CHAMPIONS LEAGUE: Players

GOAL RACE

Rivals Cristiano Ronaldo and Lionel Messi top the all-time UEFA Champions League scoring charts. Ronaldo has scored 105 goals for Real Madrid and Manchester United (including qualifying). Messi has 94 goals, all for Barcelona, and both players have struck hat-tricks seven times in the competition. Spanish striker Raúl González is in third place with 71 goals.

NOTABLE GOALS

In the last minute of added time in a 2009-10 group game, Sinan Bolat's headed goal (*right*) for Standard Liège against AZ Alkmaar made him the first keeper to score in open play. In 2014, Roma's Francesco Totti became the oldest Champions League goalscorer when the 38-year-old struck for Roma against CSKA. In 2011-12, against Bayer Leverkusen, Lionel Messi became the first player since 1979 to score five goals in a game.

SUPER-FAST STRIKES

The quickest Champions League goal was scored by Bayern Munich's Roy Makaay (*right*) after just 10.12 seconds in 2006-07. Two seasons earlier, veteran defender Paolo Maldini scored the fastest goal in a final, slotting home after just 52 seconds for AC Milan versus Liverpool.

QUICKEST HAT-TRICK

Over 100 hat-tricks have been scored in the UEFA Champions League since 1992. The fastest took Bafétimbi Gomis just seven minutes to complete in 2011 as Olympique Lyonnais beat Dinamo Zagreb 7-1.

Lionel Messi scored twice in Barcelona's 2014-15 semi-final first leg win against Bayern Munich. The striker has notched seven Champions League hat-tricks, tied at the top with Cristiano Ronaldo.

MOST CHAMPIONS LEAGUE APPEARANCES

Player	Games	Team
Iker Casillas	168	Porto, Real Madrid
Xavi	157	Barcelona
Ryan Giggs	151	Manchester United
Raúl	144	FC Schalke 04, Real Madrid
Cristiano Ronaldo	144	Real Madrid, Manchester United

SEEING RED

Patrick Vieira, Edgar Davids, Zlatan Ibrahimović and Didier Drogba have all been sent off a record three times in Champions League games. Drogba is one of only three players to be sent off in the final (2008), the others being Jens Lehmann (2006) and Juventus midfielder Juan Cuadrado (2017).

UEFA CHAMPIONS LEAGUE: Other records

DOUBLE HAT-TRICK

Nineteen managers have claimed European club football's greatest prize on two occasions, but only two have lifted the trophy three times. Bob Paisley coached Liverpool to glory in 1977, 1978 and 1981, while Carlo Ancelotti took AC Milan to two UEFA Champions League triumphs (2003, 2007) and Real Madrid to one (2014).

CUP DEFENDERS

Ten managers have led their side to a successful defence of the European Cup: Jose Villalonga (Real Madrid, 1956 and 1957); Luis Carniglia (Real Madrid, 1958 and 1959); Bela Guttmann (Benfica, 1961 and 1962); Helenio Herrera (Inter Milan, 1964 and 1965); Stefan Kovacs (Ajax, 1972 and 1973); Dettmar Cramer (Bayern Munich, 1975 and 1976), Bob Paisley (Liverpool, 1977 and 1978); Brian Clough (Nottingham Forest, 1979 and 1980); and Arrigo Sacchi (AC Milan, 1989 and 1990). Zinedine Zidane is the only coach to have performed the same feat in the Champions League era, with Real Madrid in 2016 and 2017.

When Jose Mourinho won the UEFA Champions League with Inter Milan in 2010, his team became the first to win the treble of Italian league title, Coppa Italia and Champions League.

DIFFERENT CLUB, SAME RESULT

Ernst Happel (*far right*) led Feyenoord to the European crown in 1970 and Hamburger SV to the title in 1983 to become the first manager to win with two different clubs. Four others – Jupp Heynckes, Ottmar Hitzfeld, Jose Mourinho and Carlo Ancelotti – have matched his achievement.

FAMILIAR FINAL FEELING

Four managers hold the record for the most appearances (four) in a UEFA Champions League final: Miguel Muñoz (Real Madrid in 1960, 1962, 1964 and 1966); Marcello Lippi (Juventus in 1996, 1997, 1998 and 2003); Sir Alex Ferguson (Manchester United in 1999, 2008, 2009 and 2011); and Carlo Ancelotti (AC Milan in 2003, 2005, 2007 and Real Madrid in 2014).

JOSE KNOWS

Jose Mourinho is the only manager in UEFA Champions League history to reach the semi-final of the competition with four different teams. The Portuguese coach achieved the feat with Porto in 2004, Chelsea in 2005 and 2007, Inter Milan in 2010 and with Real Madrid in 2011, 2012 and 2013. He won the trophy in 2004 and 2010.

MOST EUROPEAN CUP/CHAMPIONS LEAGUE MATCHES AS MANAGER

Manager	Matches
Sir Alex Ferguson	209
Arsène Wenger	201
Carlo Ancelotti	158
Mircea Lucescu	131
Jose Mourinho	127

LEAGUES AROUND THE WORLD

Every country that competes in world football has a domestic league in which its top clubs compete for the glory of winning the league title. Even the tiny Pacific island nation of Tuvalu has its eight-team A Division, despite the country's total population of less than 11,000 being able to fit easily into an average-size football stadium! While the game first developed in Europe, strong leagues can now be found on all continents, including Japan's J.League, Brazil's Campeonato and Major League Soccer in the USA and Canada.

Ulsan Hyundai (*in blue*) and Pohang Steelers finished runners-up and champions in the 2013 Korean K-League, giving the Steelers their fifth title – two behind record-holders Seongnam FC. Jeonbuk Hyundai Motors won back-to-back titles in 2014 and 2015.

BRAZIL: Campeonato

 ## CAMPEONATO CHAMPIONS

Seventeen clubs have won Brazil's top league. Palmeiras are the leading team with nine titles. Only two teams have won three or more championships in a row: Santos (five in a row from 1961) and São Paulo (2006, 2007 and 2008). The biggest ever crowd at a Brazilian league match was in 1983, when 155,523 fans packed into the Maracanã Stadium in Rio de Janeiro to watch Flamengo defeat Santos 3-0.

 ## MOST GOALS IN A SEASON

Washington Stecanela Cerqueira (*above*) signed for Atlético Paranaense in 2004 and made an immediate impact. His 34 goals made him the season's top scorer and the record goal getter in any Brazilian championship season. Washington also topped the table in 2008 with 21 goals for Fluminense.

ROGÉRIO'S RECORDS

Rogério Ceni holds two amazing records that may not be broken for a long time. The goalkeeper made his Brazilian league debut for São Paulo in 1993 and by the time he retired in December 2015 he had notched up 575 league appearances – over 100 more than the second-placed player. Ceni's free kicks and penalties brought him 65 Brazilian league goals – a record for a keeper – and over 120 goals overall for São Paulo.

DYNAMITE DINAMITE

Roberto Dinamite (real name Carlos Roberto de Oliveira) played almost all his career for Vasco da Gama and scored an all-time record 190 goals in the top flight of the Brazilian league between 1971 and 1993 – 36 goals more than the second-highest scorer, Romário.

A SEASON OF CHANGES

The 2015 Campeonato, won by Corinthians, saw more than 30 managerial changes in the 20-team league, with Goiás and São Paulo each having four different coaches during the season. Vanderlei Luxemburgo, the league's most successful manager with five titles, was sacked twice – first in his fourth spell at Flamengo in May and then from Cruzeiro in August.

Two of Brazil's most successful clubs in action – Flamengo (*left*, six titles) and Santos (eight titles). They are two of the five sides never to have been relegated to Brazil's second division, alongside Cruzeiro, São Paolo and Internacional.

USA: Major League Soccer

MLS CUP WINNERS

The Los Angeles Galaxy is the most successful team in the MLS with five MLS Cups (awarded to teams who win the championship final game), the latest win coming in 2014 with a 2-1 victory over the New England Revolution (*below*). They are followed by DC United with four MLS Cup victories.

RECORD FEES

In the past, many of the best footballers in MLS were transferred to clubs in Europe or Central and South America. Recently, some former MLS stars have returned. Clint Dempsey's US$9.7-million move from Tottenham Hotspur to Seattle Sounders in 2013 was the record transfer into MLS before Toronto FC bought Michael Bradley from Serie A side Roma for US$10 million in 2014.

MOST CAREER GOALS IN MLS

Player	Goals	Games
Landon Donovan	145	340
Jeff Cunningham	134	365
Jaime Moreno	133	340
Chris Wondolowski	127	274
Ante Razov	114	262

CLEAN-SHEET KINGS

Goalkeeper Kevin Hartman, who retired in 2013, has played more minutes in MLS (37,260) than any other player. His tally of 112 clean sheets is second in the MLS all-time list behind Real Salt Lake's Nick Rimando, who has reached 132 clean sheets in 434 games.

REGULAR SEASON WINNERS

Teams who top the regular MLS season league win the Supporters' Shield, but going on to lift the MLS Cup has proved a tough task with, in the first 21 seasons, only six regular season-league toppers winning the MLS Cup.

Diego Valeri (*in green*) of the Portland Timbers was voted Most Valuable Player in the 2015 MLS Cup final as his side beat Columbus Crew 2-1 to win the trophy for the first time. Valeri opened the scoring after just 27 seconds, the fastest goal in MLS Cup history.

WINNING STREAK

In September 1997, the Los Angeles Galaxy began a record 14-game winning streak that lasted until May 1998. It included a 7-4 victory over the Colorado Rapids – the highest-scoring game in MLS history. A few weeks after the run ended, the Galaxy bounced back to record the biggest ever MLS win, defeating Dallas Burn 8-1.

POOR PERFORMANCE

In the 2005 season, Chivas USA won just four games – a record low at the time. DC United eclipsed them in 2013, managing just three wins all season.

JAPAN: J.League

EVER PRESENT

Following Nagoya Grampus' relegation in 2016, only two teams have taken part in every J.League Division 1 season since the competition kicked off in 1993: Kashima Antlers and Yokohama F. Marinos, whose Nissan Stadium is the league's largest with a capacity of 72,370.

In March 2017, Kazuyoshi Miura extended his record as Japan's oldest goalscorer. He was 50 years and 14 days old when he scored the winner for Yokohama FC against Thespakusatsu Gunma.

J.LEAGUE TOP SCORERS BY YEAR

Year	Player	Goals	Club
2011	Joshua Kennedy	19	Nagoya Grampus
2012	Hisato Satō	22	Sanfrecce Hiroshima
2013	Yoshito Okubo	26	Kawasaki Frontale
2014	Yoshito Okubo	18	Kawasaki Frontale
2015	Yoshito Okubo	23	Kawasaki Frontale
2016	Peter Utaka	19	Sanfrecce Hiroshima
	Leandro	19	Vissel Kobe

TWELVE-GOAL THRILLER

The most goals in a J.League game occurred in 1998 when Kashiwa Reysol won 7-5 away at Cerezo Osaka's Nagai Stadium. This beat the record set the previous year when Kashiwa had lost 7-4 to Bellmare Hiratsuka (now known as Shonan Bellmare).

CHAMPIONS

MAGICAL MASASHI

Masashi Nakayama made his J.League debut in 1994 and until 2009 was a regular in the Júbilo Iwata side. He scored 157 J.League goals – more than any other player – including a record 36 league goals in the 1998 season, a tally which included an unprecedented five hat-tricks. After a short spell with Consadole Sapporo, Nakayama retired in 2012 at the age of 45.

CHAMPION CLUBS

Nine clubs have won the J.League. The most recent back-to-back champions are Sanfrecce Hiroshima, whose win in 2013 made them the fourth different team to successfully defend the title. Overall, Kashima Antlers and Sanfrecce Hiroshima are the league's most successful clubs with eight titles.

LONGEST HEADED GOAL

In a 2011 J.League Division 2 match against Yokohama FC, Fagiano Okayama FC's Ryujiro Ueda headed the ball powerfully out of his own half and watched in disbelief as the ball bounced up and over the opposition goalkeeper and into the net. Ueda's long-distance goal was measured at 57.8 metres.

The 2014 J.League's Most Valuable Player, Yasuhito Endo, lifts the league trophy as Gamba Osaka win their second J.League title. Gamba were relegated in 2012 but bounced back up the following year. In 2014 they took the title by one point from Urawa Red Diamonds.

OTHER league records

 ## CHINESE SUPER LEAGUE

Seven teams have been champions of the Chinese Super League, which began in 1994 as the Jia-A League. Dalian Shide are the most successful, with eight titles (including two hat-tricks), whilst Guangzhou Evergrande have dominated recently, winning six titles in a row (2011 to 2016).

 ## LOW-SCORING CHAMPIONS

In 1998, AIK became champions of Allsvenskan, Sweden's top league, despite scoring just 25 goals in 26 matches – a tally lower than all 13 of their rivals. In the 2009-10 Ghana Premier League, newly-promoted Aduana Stars scored just 19 goals in 30 games, but won the title thanks to eight 1-0 victories.

 ## LIGA MX

The top league in Mexico – the Primera División, or Liga MX – is always highly competitive and has been won by Club América and Guadalajara a record 12 times. Toluca are two championship wins behind the pair.

 ## AUSTRALIAN A-LEAGUE

The first season of the A-League, in 2005-06, saw an unenviable record, as New Zealand Knights won just one out of 21 games. The most wins in a season is 20 by Sydney FC (left, in light blue) in 2016-17 on the way to the club's third championship final win. Melbourne City scored a record 63 league goals in 2015-16.

⚽ ARGENTINIAN PRIMERA DIVISIÓN

River Plate (*below, in white*) are Argentina's most successful side, winning over 30 league titles. Two strikers, Arsenio Erico for Independiente and River Plate's Ángel Labruna, are the Primera's top scorers, each with 293 goals. The youngest player to appear in the Primera is Sergio Agüero, who debuted for Independiente in 2003 at the age of 15 years, 35 days.

Peñarol's Jonathan Rodriguez attempts to shield the ball from Nacional's Diego Arismendi. The two clubs are Uruguay's most successful, with Nacional having won 46 Primera División titles to Peñarol's 50.

⚽ MOST TITLES

In South America, Peñarol have been crowned Uruguayan league champions a record 50 times. The most frequently crowned league champions in Africa are Egypt's Al-Ahly, with 39 titles. In Asia, South China have dominated long periods of the Hong Kong First Division League, winning 41 league titles.

INTERNATIONAL CLUB COMPETITIONS

Five of the six footballing continents have their own Champions League, in which the best teams from different countries are pitted against each other, while South America has the Copa Libertadores competition for 38 clubs. The winners of each of these six international club competitions do battle in a short tournament known as the FIFA Club World Cup.

Europe has had a number of club competitions in addition to the UEFA Champions League. They include the Intertoto Cup (1961-2008), the Cup Winners' Cup (1960-99) and the Inter-Cities Fairs Cup. The latter began in 1955 and was replaced by the UEFA Cup in 1971, which itself became the UEFA Europa League in 2009.

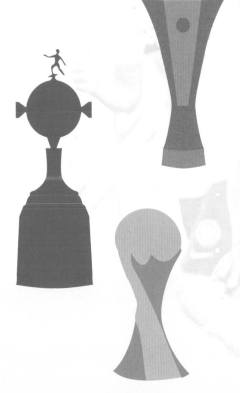

Western Sydney Wanderers and Guangzhou Evergrande battle it out in the 2015 Asian Champions League. Guangzhou became the first Chinese side to win the competition, in 2013, while Western Sydney Wanderers won the 2014 Champions League on their debut in the competition.

UEFA EUROPA LEAGUE

ALL OVER EUROPE

UEFA Cup/Europa League winners have come from 11 countries, from Portugal in the west (Porto in 2003, 2011) to eastern nations such as Russia (Zenit St. Petersburg in 2008) and Ukraine (Shakhtar Donetsk in 2009). Spanish teams have won the title a record ten times.

EUROPA GOAL FEST

Many rounds of the tournament are played over two games, home and away. The highest aggregate win, in 1972, saw Dutch side Feyenoord defeat Rumelange of Luxembourg 9-0 at home and 12-0 away for a 21-0 aggregate score. Another Luxembourg club, Red Boys Differdange, suffered the worst single-leg drubbing – a 14-0 defeat to Ajax in 1984, with Marco van Basten scoring five.

SCORE AND PASS

Henrik Larsson is the competition's leading scorer with 40 goals in 56 games for Feyenoord, Celtic and Helsingborg. Another of Larsson's former clubs, Manchester United, won their first Europa League crown in 2017, defeating Ajax 2-0 with goals from Henrikh Mkhitaryan and Paul Pogba (right) who ended the competition as its most successful passer with 863 passes completed.

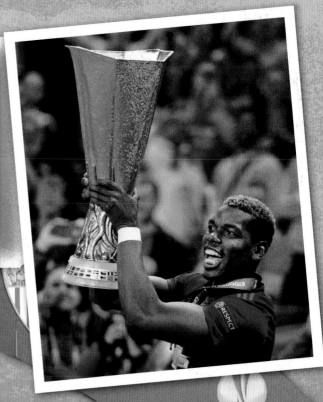

MOST APPEARANCES IN THE UEFA CUP/EUROPA LEAGUE

Player	Games
Giuseppe Bergomi	96
Frank Rost	90
Dimitris Salpingidis	76
Mladen Petrić	72
João Pereira	71
Walter Zenga	69

Sevilla celebrate with the Europa League trophy in 2014. They had to go through two qualifying rounds at the start of the competition, beating both opponents 9-1 on aggregate.

SUPER SEVILLA

In May 2016, Sevilla's 3-1 win in the final over Liverpool thanks to two goals from Coke and one from Kévin Gameiro meant that the Spanish club had won three Europa Leagues in a row. Added to their back-to-back triumphs in 2006 and 2007, Sevilla's five cup wins place them two ahead of Juventus (1977, 1990, 1993), Inter Milan (1991, 1994, 1998) and Liverpool (1973, 1976, 2001).

COPA LIBERTADORES

BIG THREE

Teams from the 'Big Three' footballing countries in South America (Argentina, Brazil and Uruguay) have won 49 of the 56 Copa Libertadores competitions. Most successful of all are Independiente from Argentina, who have won all seven of the finals they have reached (1964-65, 1972-75 and 1984).

San Lorenzo's players celebrate after lifting the Copa Libertadores trophy in 2014 for the first time. Néstor Ortigoza's penalty gave the Argentinian side a second-leg victory after the first leg was drawn 1-1.

Neymar, playing for Santos, celebrates one of his eight goals in the 2012 Copa, making him that year's joint leading scorer with Matías Alustiza of Ecuador's Deportivo Quito.

EVER READY

Ever Hugo Almeida, the long-serving goalkeeper of Paraguay's Club Olimpia, appeared in a record 113 Copa games between 1973 and 1990. In his 70th Copa game, versus Estudiantes in 1984, Almeida even scored the winning goal, a penalty.

FREQUENT FINALISTS

Uruguayan club Peñarol and Boca Juniors of Argentina have reached the Copa final a record ten times. Club Olimpia of Paraguay are the most successful club from outside the Big Three nations. They were champions in 1979, 1990 and 2002, and have been runners-up four times, most recently in 2013.

COPA SURPRISES

The 2016 Copa was full of shocks, with 2015 champions River Plate of Argentina knocked out in the Round of 16 by Independiente del Valle. The Ecuadorians went on to defeat heavyweights UNAM from Mexico and Boca Juniors to reach the final. There, they were defeated by 1989 champions Atlético Nacional from Colombia (right), in the first final not to feature teams from Argentina, Brazil, Uruguay or Paraguay.

MOST CAREER GOALS IN THE COPA LIBERTADORES

Player	Goals	Clubs
Alberto Spencer	54	Peñarol, Barcelona SC
Fernando Morena	37	Peñarol
Pedro Virgilio Rocha	36	Peñarol, São Paulo, Palmeiras
Daniel Onega	31	River Plate
Julio Morales	30	Nacional

FASTEST GOAL, MOST GOALS

Felix Suárez struck after just six seconds for Alianza Lima of Peru against Santa Fe in 1976 – the tournament's fastest goal. Nine years later, Juan Carlos Sánchez scored a record six times in Club Blooming of Bolivia's 8-0 mauling of Venezuelan side Deportivo Italia – the most goals by a player in a single game.

FIFA CLUB WORLD CUP

EARLY CHAMPIONS

A competition for champion clubs from different continents has been held since 1960, when Real Madrid defeated Peñarol of Uruguay 5-1 over two matches. The Intercontinental Cup ran from 1960 to 2004 and pitted the two champion clubs of South America and Europe against each other. Five clubs – Nacional, Peñarol, Boca Juniors, AC Milan and Real Madrid – won the competition three times.

GOING GLOBAL

From 2000, the tournament invited the champions of all six continents, with South American and European teams entering at the semi-final stage. The host country is also granted a place. In 2000, hosts Brazil fielded two clubs (Vasco da Gama and Corinthians) who both reached the final, with Corinthians winning 4-3 on penalties.

AWESOME AUCKLAND

Auckland City of New Zealand have reached a record nine FIFA Club World Cups, followed by Egypt's Al-Ahly with five. All but one of the teams that have represented CONCACAF (Central and North America) have been Mexican – the exception being Costa Rica's Deportivo Saprissa in 2005.

Barcelona's Luis Suárez holds off River Plate's Matías Kranevitter in the 2015 final. Suárez scored twice in the 3-0 win, topping the tournament scoring table and helping Barça to their fifth trophy out of a possible six in 2015.

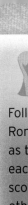

GOALS GALORE

Following a goal spree at the 2016 competition, Cristiano Ronaldo joined Luis Suárez, Lionel Messi and César Delgado as the FIFA Club World Cup's leading scorers with five goals each. Barcelona, the club that Messi and Suárez play for, have scored 23 goals in the competition – seven more than any other side – while their former coach Pep Guardiola is the only manager to have won the tournament three times.

FIFA CLUB WORLD CUP CHAMPIONS

2000	Corinthians (Brazil)
2005	São Paulo (Brazil)
2006	Internacional (Brazil)
2007	AC Milan (Italy)
2008	Manchester United (England)
2009	Barcelona (Spain)
2010	Inter Milan (Italy)
2011	Barcelona (Spain)
2012	Corinthians (Brazil)
2013	Bayern Munich (Germany)
2014	Real Madrid (Spain)
2015	Barcelona (Spain)
2016	Real Madrid (Spain)

AFRICA ACTION

In 2010, TP Mazembe from the Democratic Republic of Congo became the first African club to reach the tournament's final. They were followed three years later by Raja Casablanca from Morocco, who lost 2-0 in the final to Bayern Munich – the first German side to appear at the tournament.

PART 2: International Football

The first ever official football match between national teams was played in 1872, when Scotland and England battled to a 0-0 draw in front of a crowd of around 4,000.

Today, over 200 countries pick their best players to take part in matches against international opposition. They compete in friendly games, qualification matches, competitions held on their own continent, or at the biggest global competition, the FIFA World Cup. While attempting to qualify for the 2002 FIFA World Cup, Australia recorded the biggest scoreline in international football, defeating American Samoa 31-0 with 13 goals from striker Archie Thompson.

Australia's James Troisi battles with South Korean defenders in the final of the 2015 AFC Asian Cup. Troisi scored the winner in the 105th minute to give Australia their first Asian Cup title.

FIFA WORLD CUP

The most glittering prize in football, the FIFA World Cup, is held once every four years. It was first hosted in Uruguay in 1930, when just 13 nations took part. By the time of the 21st tournament, 208 teams contested qualifying games in the hope of becoming one of the 32 elite sides in Russia for the 2018 competition. Over the years, the FIFA World Cup has thrown up drama, controversy and plenty of stunning goals, including a record 171 at both the 1998 and 2014 tournaments and a total of 2,379, the last being Mario Götze's 113th-minute winner in the 2014 final.

Germany's epic 7-1 thrashing of hosts Brazil in the 2014 FIFA World Cup semi-finals was the first time any team has scored seven goals in a semi. Germany's first five goals came in just 29 minutes, the quickest ever at a FIFA World Cup.

FIFA WORLD CUP: Teams 1

 GOLDEN DAYS

Brazil have won the FIFA World Cup five times – more than any other country. They are also the only side to have appeared at every tournament and have gone through seven of them unbeaten (1958, 1962, 1970, 1978, 1986, 1994, 2002). Brazil played in white shirts until a shock defeat to Uruguay in the 1950 FIFA World Cup final, after which they changed to their famous gold shirts and blue shorts.

 SPANISH SUCCESS

When Spain triumphed in South Africa in 2010, they became only the third side after Brazil and Argentina to win the FIFA World Cup away from their home continent (Germany became the fourth in 2014). Spain's tally of eight goals was the lowest ever by the champion team and six fewer than the number of goals West Germany let in on their way to lifting the trophy in 1954 – the most conceded by any champions.

FIFA WORLD CUP WINNERS

5	Brazil (1958, 1962, 1970, 1994, 2002)
4	Germany/W. Germany (1954, 1974, 1990, 2014)
4	Italy (1934, 1938, 1982, 2006)
2	Argentina (1978, 1986)
2	Uruguay (1930, 1950)
1	England (1966)
1	France (1998)
1	Spain (2010)

EURO PIONEERS

Germany started the 2014 FIFA World Cup with a bang, beating Portugal 4-0 and cruising unbeaten through their group. Narrow victories over Algeria (2-1) and France (1-0) saw them progress to the semi-finals, where they scored seven of their 18 tournament goals to knock out Brazil. A gripping final against Argentina saw chances at both ends before Mario Götze (*below*) scored the winner in extra time. Joachim Löw's side became the first European team to win the World Cup on South American soil.

 # FIRST STRIKES

FIFA World Cup hosts have scored the opening goal at five tournaments. In 2014, host nation Brazil's Marcelo struck the first goal, but it was an own goal to give Croatia the lead. Mexico conceded the FIFA World Cup's first ever goal, scored by Lucien Laurent for France in 1930.

 # SHOCK EXITS

Famous FIFA World Cup shocks include Argentina losing to Cameroon in 1990 and France's loss to Senegal in 2002, when France also became the first holders to be knocked out without scoring a goal. Spain didn't fare much better at the 2014 tournament, exiting the competition after just two games when they were beaten 5-1 by the Netherlands and 2-0 by Chile (*left*).

FIFA WORLD CUP: Teams 2

 FREQUENT FINALISTS

The Netherlands have appeared in three FIFA World Cup finals (1974, 1978 and 2010, *above*) without winning the competition. Germany or West Germany have been runners-up on four occasions and have made a record eight appearances in the final, one ahead of Brazil.

 BIG WINS

The biggest win at a FIFA World Cup was in 1982, when Hungary thrashed El Salvador 10-1. The Hungarians starred in another 11-goal game in 1954, beating West Germany 8-3. At the same tournament, Switzerland's 7-5 thriller against Austria saw the most goals scored in a FIFA World Cup game.

REACHING THE WORLD CUP

Competition for a place at the tournament is fierce and over 130 countries have so far tried and failed to reach a FIFA World Cup. In 2014, Bosnia and Herzegovina became the latest FIFA World Cup debutant. Since the 1940s, the highest placing by a country making their debut is third (Portugal in 1966 and Croatia in 1998).

Argentina's captain, Lionel Messi, moves in to tackle Zvjezdan Misimović of Bosnia and Herzegovina in their group game at the 2014 FIFA World Cup. Messi was awarded the Golden Ball as the player of the tournament.

SCOLARI'S RUN

Brazil, coached by Luiz Felipe Scolari, began a winning run at the 2002 FIFA World Cup, the only tournament to be hosted by two nations (South Korea and Japan), that continued for 11 games until the quarter-finals of the 2006 tournament. Scolari was reappointed coach of Brazil for the 2014 tournament, but stepped down after heavy defeats to Germany and the Netherlands.

A WAIT FOR A WIN

Bulgaria had to wait until their sixth FIFA World Cup and play 17 games without winning before they recorded their first victory in the competition. A 4-0 defeat of Greece in 1994 was the start of a winning spree for Bulgaria, who beat Argentina and then knocked out Mexico and reigning champions Germany to finish fourth.

FIFA WORLD CUP: Players 1

 ## SPEEDY STRIKES

In the third-place play-off game of the 2002 FIFA World Cup, Turkey's Hakan Şükür (*left, in white*) scored 11 seconds after kick-off against South Korea to register the FIFA World Cup's fastest ever goal. The fastest goal of all came in qualifying for the 2018 competition when Belgium's Christian Benteke scored after just 8.1 seconds in a 6-0 win over Gibraltar.

 ## MIROSLAV'S MAGIC

Both Ronaldo of Brazil (in 2006) and Germany's Miroslav Klose (in 2014) scored their 15th FIFA World Cup goals against Ghana. Klose went one better, scoring in the 23rd minute of the 2014 semi-final versus Brazil to become the all-time leading goalscorer at the FIFA World Cup finals.

FIFA WORLD CUP TOP SCORERS

Player	Country	FIFA World Cups	Goals
Miroslav Klose	Germany	2002, 2006, 2010, 2014	16
Ronaldo	Brazil	1998, 2002, 2006	15
Gerd Müller	Germany	1970, 1974	14
Just Fontaine	France	1958	13
Pelé	Brazil	1958, 1962, 1966, 1970	12

QUALIFYING FEATS

In over 6,400 qualification games, no team has played more than Mexico's 163 matches and no player has scored more goals than Iran's Ali Daei, with 35 goals in four qualifying campaigns. Four of Daei's goals were scored against the Maldives during 1998 FIFA World Cup qualification. During that campaign the Maldives conceded a record 59 goals in just six games.

YOUNG GUN

Edson Arantes do Nascimento is better known to the world as Pelé. He is the only player to have won three FIFA World Cups (1958, 1962 and 1970). In ten days during the 1958 finals (*above*), the 17-year-old Brazilian set three goal records: becoming the competition's youngest goalscorer with his strike against Wales, the youngest hat-trick scorer versus France and the youngest goalscorer in a final – against Sweden.

German striker Miroslav Klose celebrates scoring his record-breaking 16th FIFA World Cup goal, against Brazil. Klose has scored more goals for Germany than any other player – 71, three ahead of Gerd Müller.

FIVE-TIMERS

Only two men have played in five FIFA World Cups. Mexico's goalkeeper Antonio Carbajal went to five tournaments in a row (1950-66), playing 11 matches but conceding 25 goals – an unwanted record matched by Saudi Arabia's Mohamed al-Deayea in 2002. The other five-timer is German midfielder Lothar Matthäus, who holds the record for the most appearances at FIFA World Cups – 25 games in total.

FIFA WORLD CUP: Players 2

KEEPING RECORDS

Two keepers hold the record for the most FIFA World Cup clean sheets. Both Peter Shilton (1982, 1986, 1990) and Fabien Barthez (1998, 2002, 2006) played in ten games without conceding. Swiss keeper Pascal Zuberbühler (*left*) didn't let in a single goal in regular or extra-time in 2006. In contrast, Hong Duk-Yung let in 16 goals in just two games during South Korea's FIFA World Cup debut in 1954.

YOUNG AND OLD

When Norman Whiteside played for Northern Ireland against Yugoslavia at the 1982 FIFA World Cup, he became the competition's youngest ever player, aged 17 years and 41 days. Tony Meola was the youngest ever captain at age 21 when he skippered the USA against Czechoslovakia in 1990. In 2014, keeper Faryd Mondragon became the oldest ever player at 43 years and 3 days when he came on as a substitute in Colombia's 4-1 win over Japan.

HAT-TRICK HEROES

Four players have scored two hat-tricks at the FIFA World Cup. Sándor Kocsis (1954), Just Fontaine (1958) and Gerd Müller (1974) all scored them in one tournament, while Gabriel Batistuta bagged his against Greece in 1994 and versus Jamaica in 1998. The only substitute to score a hat-trick was Hungary's László Kiss in 1982. His three goals in eight minutes were also the fastest in FIFA World Cup history.

 # OH BROTHER

Over 50 pairs of brothers have played at a FIFA World Cup, but only two pairs for different teams – Jérôme Boateng (Germany) and Derek Boateng (Ghana) in 2010, and Jérôme Boateng and Kevin-Prince Boateng (Ghana) in 2014 (*left*). Two pairs of brothers have won a FIFA World Cup final: Fritz and Ottmar Walter of West Germany in 1954 and England's Jack and Bobby Charlton in 1966.

 ## A GOAL EVERY GAME

Two players have scored in six FIFA World Cup games in a row at a single tournament – Just Fontaine for France in 1958 and Jairzinho for Brazil in 1970. James Rodriguez went close, scoring a goal in each of Colombia's five games at the 2014 FIFA World Cup. Fontaine's goal total of 13 is the most by a player at a single World Cup.

Roger Milla scores for Cameroon against Russia at the 1994 FIFA World Cup. Milla was 42 years and 39 days old, making him the oldest World Cup goalscorer.

 ## AWESOME OLEG

The most goals scored by a player in a single game was Oleg Salenko's five for Russia against Cameroon in 1994. Ernest Wilimowski scored four for Poland in a 1938 game, yet ended up on the losing side as Brazil triumphed 6-5.

FIFA WORLD CUP: Other records

FOREIGN COACHES

No team has achieved FIFA World Cup glory when led by a foreign coach. Even so, 14 of the 32 coaches at the 2014 FIFA World Cup were not from the country they were managing. They included Italian Fabio Capello (Russia), German Jurgen Klinsmann (USA, *left*) and Argentinians José Pékerman (Colombia) and Jorge Sampaoli (Chile).

SUCCESSFUL SUPREMOS

Vittorio Pozzo masterminded Italy's back-to-back FIFA World Cup wins in 1934 and 1938, and is the only coach to have won two FIFA World Cups. Two men have won the tournament as a player and later as a coach – Germany's Franz Beckenbauer (1974 and 1990) and Mario Zagallo of Brazil (1958 and 1962 as a player, 1970 as coach).

SIX-CUP CARLOS

Helmut Schön coached West Germany for four FIFA World Cups and a record 25 games. They finished runners-up in 1966, third in 1970 and were champions in 1974. Brazilian Carlos Alberto Parreira is the only coach to take teams to six FIFA World Cups, including Kuwait in 1982, Brazil (in 1994 and 2006) and South Africa in 2010.

MOST GAMES AS REF

With his four refereeing appearances in 2014 to go with his five in 2010, Ravshan Irmatov from Uzbekistan has officiated the most FIFA World Cup matches. Three referees are on eight games: France's Joël Quiniou, Mexico's Benito Archundia and Uruguay's Jorge Larrionda.

RAPID REDS

The fastest red card at a FIFA World Cup came in 1986, when Uruguayan defender José Batista fouled Scotland's Gordon Strachan and was sent off after just 56 seconds. At the 2002 tournament, Argentina's Claudio Caniggia (*right*) was sent off even before he had got on the pitch, for swearing at ref Ali Bujsaim during a match against Sweden.

FOUL FEST

At the 2006 FIFA World Cup, Russian ref Valentin Ivanov showed a record 16 yellow and four red cards in a feisty Portugal v Netherlands game. Portugal received nine of the yellow cards, and share the record for the most cards received by a team in one game with the Netherlands, who were also shown nine yellows in the 2010 final.

Valentin Ivanov shows Portugal's Costinha his second yellow card during the record-breaking 2006 game against the Netherlands. Costinha was one of four players sent off, another World Cup record.

FIFA WORLD CUP: Other records 2

HOSTING THE CUP

In 2014 Brazil (*left*) became the fifth nation to host the FIFA World Cup twice, the others being Mexico (1970 and 1986), Italy (1934 and 1990), France (1938 and 1998) and Germany (1974 and 2006). Colombia originally won the right to host the 1986 FIFA World Cup but pulled out in 1982 due to financial problems.

PENALTY SHOOTOUTS

The first penalty shootout to decide a drawn game was at the 1982 FIFA World Cup. Germany beat France 5-4 and now have the best shootout record, winning all four of their shootouts. England (*right*) have the worst record, with three losses out of three. Two FIFA World Cup finals have gone to penalties and both featured Italy, who lost to Brazil in 1994 but triumphed over France in 2006.

LONG TIME COMING

The record for the biggest gap between FIFA World Cups is held by Elba de Pádua Lima, better known as Tim. The Brazilian appeared at the 1938 FIFA World Cup as a player and then, 44 years later, at the 1982 tournament as the coach of Peru.

HIGHS AND LOWS

The lowest attendance at a FIFA World Cup match was in 1930, when a reported crowd of just 300 turned up to see Romania beat Peru 3-1. The 1950 FIFA World Cup final drew the competition's biggest crowd. The official attendance at the Maracanã was given as 173,850, but reports suggest there were close to 200,000 spectators.

TOP FIFA WORLD CUP TOTAL ATTENDANCES

Attendance	Host	Year
3,587,538	USA	1994
3,429,873	Brazil	2014
3,359,439	Germany	2006
3,178,856	South Africa	2010
2,785,100	France	1998

INNOVATIONS

The first tournament to feature red and yellow cards was the 1970 FIFA World Cup, but a player wasn't sent off until 1974. The 2014 FIFA World Cup was the first to feature goal-line technology to determine whether the whole of the ball had crossed the line. It was also the first in which referees used vanishing spray to mark the line to which the defending team must retreat for a free kick (*left*).

UEFA EUROPEAN CHAMPIONSHIP

A Europe-wide competition for the continent's national teams was discussed for decades before the first UEFA European Championship kicked off in 1958. Held once every four years, the early championships featured qualifying rounds over a long period leading to just four teams competing in a finals tournament. The number of teams at the finals increased to eight in 1980 and 16 in 1996. The 2016 tournament in France featured 24 teams for the first time. Germany (or West Germany) have made it to the most finals tournaments – 12, including every one since 1972. The Germans, along with the 2012 champions, Spain, have won the competition a record three times.

Portugal celebrate their first international trophy at EURO 2016 after defeating France 1-0 with a goal from substitute striker Éder in extra-time. Their run to the final means they have reached at least the semi-finals in five out of the seven EUROs they have played in.

UEFA EUROPEAN CHAMPIONSHIP: Teams

GOAL AVALANCHE

The highest-scoring finals game was Yugoslavia's 5-4 win over France in 1960. The Yugoslavs also lost 6-1 to the Netherlands in 2000, one of the biggest defeats. Germany's 13-0 mauling of San Marino during EURO 2008 qualifying remains a record. San Marino hold another unwanted record, having lost 59 EURO qualifiers in a row until a 0-0 draw with Estonia in November 2014.

SHOOTOUTS

There have been 18 games decided by penalty shootouts at the EUROs. England and the Netherlands have each lost a record three out of four. Only the Czech Republic (three shootouts) and Turkey (one shootout in 2008, *above*) boast a perfect record.

MOST GOALS, FEWEST GOALS

At EURO 2000, Yugoslavia conceded a record 13 goals. Three of those were scored by Slovenia, who led 3-0 before the Yugoslavs pulled off the biggest comeback in EUROs history to draw 3-3. The most miserly team is Spain's EURO 2012 side, who conceded only one goal in six games on the way to the title.

SUPER SHOCKS

EURO 2016 brought plenty of shocks. England were beaten 2-1 by Iceland who, with a population of under 340,000, are the smallest nation ever to qualify for the finals. Wales knocked out Belgium (second in the FIFA world rankings) to become the smallest nation to reach the semi-finals. The biggest ever EUROs shock came in 2004, when unfancied Greece won the trophy despite their lowly FIFA world ranking of 35.

Iceland's Ragnar Sigurðsson is mobbed by his teammates after scoring the equaliser against England at EURO 2016. Incredibly, Iceland were ranked 131st in the world by FIFA as recently as June 2012.

UEFA EUROPEAN CHAMPIONSHIP HOSTS AND FINALISTS

Year	Host(s)	Final
1960	France	USSR 2-1 Yugoslavia
1964	Spain	Spain 2-1 USSR
1968	Italy	Italy 2-0 Yugoslavia (after replay)
1972	Belgium	West Germany 3-0 USSR
1976	Yugoslavia	Czech. 2-2 W. Germany (5-3 pens)
1980	Italy	West Germany 2-1 Belgium
1984	France	France 2-0 Spain
1988	West Germany	Netherlands 2-0 USSR
1992	Sweden	Denmark 2-0 Germany
1996	England	Germany 2-1 Czech Republic
2000	Belgium/Holland	France 2-1 Italy
2004	Portugal	Greece 1-0 Portugal
2008	Austria/Switz.	Spain 1-0 Germany
2012	Poland/Ukraine	Spain 4-0 Italy
2016	France	Portugal 1-0 France

UEFA EUROPEAN CHAMPIONSHIP: Players

APPEARANCE RECORDS

Portugal's star forward, Cristiano Ronaldo, has played in more UEFA European Championship games than any other player – 21 in total – and is the only player to have scored at four EURO tournaments. In 2016 his teammate Renato Sanches became the youngest player to reach the final, aged 18 years and 328 days. In contrast, Hungarian goalkeeper Gábor Király became the competition's oldest player at 40 years and 86 days when he played against Belgium at EURO 2016.

PERFECT PLATINI

Michel Platini's nine goals for France at EURO 84 are a record haul by a player at the UEFA European Championship – all the more impressive considering he played in midfield. Among Platini's goals was the competition's all-time fastest hat-trick, which he scored against Yugoslavia in just 18 minutes.

DISCIPLINARY MATTERS

Georgios Karagounis (*left, in white*) has notched up the most cards at the EUROs – eight yellows over three tournaments. Only one footballer, Radoslav Látal of the Czech Republic, has been sent off twice (in 1996 and 2000). The only player to have been sent off in the tournament final is France's Yvon le Roux, who received two yellow cards in 1984 against Spain.

Portugal's Cristiano Ronaldo challenges Gareth Bale of Wales in the EURO 2016 semi-finals. Ronaldo's goal in the 2-0 win extended his record for most goals scored in EURO qualifying and finals tournaments – 29 in total.

YOUNG GUN

Dutch coach Bert van Marwijk pulled a surprise at EURO 2012 by playing a teenager at full-back. Jetro Willems made his debut for the Dutch in a friendly at the end of May 2012. Less than two weeks later, the young left-back became the EUROs' youngest player – just 18 years, 71 days old.

EARLY AND LATE

In a 2004 group game between Russia and Greece, Dmitri Kirichenko scored after just 67 seconds – the EUROs' fastest ever goal. The latest goal scored came at EURO 2008, when Turkey's Semih Şentürk struck in the 120th and very last minute of extra-time against Croatia.

UEFA EUROPEAN CHAMPIONSHIP: Other records

TAILS I WIN, HEADS YOU LOSE

A coin toss was used to decide the 1968 Italy versus Soviet Union semi-final after the game ended in a 0-0 draw. The two team captains contested the toss, with Italy winning and progressing to the final versus Yugoslavia. The Italians recorded their first and only UEFA European Championship triumph with a 2-0 victory.

QUICK PENALTY

At EURO 2016, France's Paul Pogba brought down the Republic of Ireland's Shane Long in the penalty area and Robbie Brady scored the resulting spot kick just 1 minute and 58 seconds after kick-off. It was the fastest penalty in EURO history and the competition's second-fastest goal.

RECORD CROWDS

The highest and lowest crowds occurred at the same tournament in 1964. The Hungary versus Denmark game attracted a mere 3,869 spectators who rattled around the mighty Camp Nou stadium, home to Barcelona. The final, held at Real Madrid's Bernabéu stadium, saw a record 79,115 fans watch Spain beat the Soviet Union.

LONG SERVERS

Joachim Löw (with Germany, 2008-16) and Lars Lagerbäck (with Sweden, 2000-08) are the only coaches to have taken the same team to three EUROs. Lagerbäck joint-managed Iceland at EURO 2016, becoming the only person to coach at four tournaments. Anders Frisk (*right*), has refereed eight finals games, more than any other official.

Joachim Löw has taken Germany to one UEFA European Championship final (2008) and two semi-finals (2012 and 2016). He holds the record for the most EURO finals matches won as a manager – 11 in total.

VOGTS AND LÖW

Germany's Berti Vogts is the only person to have won the UEFA European Championship both as a player (1972) and as a coach (1996). His fellow German Joachim Löw holds the record for most EURO games as coach – 17 in total at EURO 2008, 2012 and 2016.

GOLDEN GOALS

At the 1996 and 2000 EUROs, golden goals were used instead of penalty shootouts to decide drawn games, with the first team to score during extra time awarded the win. A golden goal scored by France's David Trezeguet decided the EURO 2000 final versus Italy.

OTHER INTERNATIONAL COMPETITIONS

Many international competitions are held for younger players, such as the FIFA U17 World Cup, and for female footballers, including the FIFA Women's World Cup. Other international competitions are run along regional lines by the football confederation responsible for a continent. These include the Africa Cup of Nations and the CONCACAF Gold Cup, which features teams from North America, the Caribbean and Central America. While each continent has its leading footballing nations, some smaller sides still spring surprises – Tahiti winning the 2012 OFC Nations Cup, for example, or Jamaica's incredible run to the final of the 2015 CONCACAF Gold Cup.

Mexico players celebrate with the 2011 CONCACAF Gold Cup after beating the USA 4-2. They won a record seventh Gold Cup in 2015 with a 3-1 win over Jamaica.

COPA AMÉRICA

COPA HOSTS

The Copa América began in 1916 and is the oldest continental football competition. It is normally held every four years, but after Chile hosted and won the tournament for the first time in 2015, a special edition was organized to celebrate its centenary. The 2016 Copa América Centenario, held in the USA, saw a re-run of the 2015 final, with Chile again defeating Argentina on penalties. Chilean attacker Alexis Sanchez won the Golden Ball as the tournament's best player.

Chilean forward Eduardo Vargas (*in red*) was joint top scorer at the 2015 Copa, and outright top scorer in 2016 with six goals. He scored four times in Chile's 7-0 mauling of Mexico in the 2016 quarter-final.

KINGS OF THE COPA

Uruguay's 2011 Copa América victory was their 15th title, making them the most successful nation in the competition. Their 2011 campaign began with two draws, but they went on to beat Mexico, Argentina and Peru, before defeating Paraguay 3-0 in the final with goals from Diego Forlán and Luis Suárez. Forlan's father Pablo had won the Copa as a player in 1967 and his grandfather won the Copa twice as Uruguay's coach (1959 and 1967).

MOST APPEARANCES

Goalkeeper Sergio Livingstone from Chile has played a record 34 Copa América games. Two players have appeared in eight different Copa América competitions – striker Angel Romano of Uruguay and midfielder Álex Aguinaga from Ecuador (*left, in yellow*).

AWESOME ARGENTINA

Argentina have won the Copa 14 times, just one behind Uruguay. They have hosted the competition a record nine times. Argentina also hold the record for the biggest thrashings, demolishing Ecuador 12-0 in 1942 and Venezuela 11-0 in 1975. On both occasions, however, Argentina failed to win the competition.

SUPER STÁBILE

Only four coaches have ever won more than one Copa América. The undisputed king of the Copa is Guillermo Stábile, who managed Argentina to six Copa crowns (1941, 1945, 1946, 1947, 1955, 1957). As a striker, Stábile made his debut for Argentina at the 1930 FIFA World Cup, where he became the first player to score a World Cup hat-trick.

COPA AMÉRICA TOP SCORERS

Player	Goals
Norberto Méndez (Argentina)	17
Zizinho (Brazil)	17
Teodoro Fernández (Peru)	15
Severino Varela (Uruguay)	15
Ademir (Brazil)	13
Jair da Rosa Pinto (Brazil)	13
Gabriel Batistuta (Argentina)	13
José Manuel Moreno (Argentina)	13
Héctor Scarone (Uruguay)	13

AFRICA CUP OF NATIONS

FABULOUS PHARAOHS

Egypt have won the Africa Cup of Nations seven times – more than any other country. They were also responsible for the game with the most goals – a 6-3 victory over Nigeria in 1963. Nicknamed the Pharaohs, Egypt have appeared in the most tournaments (23), playing 96 matches. They have also been runners-up twice, most recently in 2017 when they lost to Cameroon.

Zambia finally won their first Africa Cup of Nations in 2012 in Gabon, just a few hundred metres from where the plane carrying the Zambian team crashed in 1993, killing 18 members of the squad.

HAIL THE HASSANS

As a player, Hassan Shehata competed for Egypt in three tournaments without lifting the trophy. As a coach, however, he is the only manager to have won three Africa Cup of Nations – a three-in-a-row feat (2006, 2008 and 2010). In 2010 one of Shehata's players, Ahmed Hassan (*right*), became the first footballer to win four Africa Cup of Nations winners' medals.

PLENTIFUL PENALTIES

The most penalty kicks needed to decide a shootout at the tournament was 24. Amazingly this has happened twice, and on both occasions Ivory Coast won. In the 1992 final they beat Ghana, while in the 2006 quarter-final they defeated Cameroon.

THE ELEPHANTS WIN

The 2015 tournament was held in Equatorial Guinea. The 2013 champions, Nigeria, failed to qualify but Ivory Coast, nicknamed the Elephants, recorded the longest gap between triumphs (23 years) by beating Ghana in the final. After a 0-0 draw, it took 22 penalties to separate the teams, with Ivory Coast winning 9-8 despite missing their first two attempts.

Ivory Coast captain Yaya Touré lifts the Africa Cup of Nations in 2015 after an epic penalty shootout against Ghana. Coach Hervé Renard became the first manager to win the trophy with two teams, following victory with Zambia in 2012.

AFRICA CUP OF NATIONS TOP SCORERS

Player	Goals
Samuel Eto'o (Cameroon)	18
Laurent Pokou (Ivory Coast)	14
Rashidi Yekeni (Nigeria)	13
Hassan El-Shazly (Egypt)	12
Didier Drogba (Ivory Coast)	11
Hossam Hassan (Egypt)	11
Patrick Mbomba (Cameroon)	11

CONCACAF GOLD CUP

Mexico's Andrés Guardado shields the ball from Rodolph Austin of Jamaica in the 2015 final. Guardado was voted player of the tournament, scoring six goals.

 ## HOME IN THE USA

The CONCACAF Gold Cup for the footballing nations of North America, Central America and the Caribbean began in 1991, when the USA beat Honduras in the final. The tournament has been hosted by the USA ever since, usually every two years, except in 1993 and 2003 when it was hosted jointly with Mexico. The reigning champions Mexico have won seven Gold Cups, followed by 2013 champions USA with five wins.

Clive Naive Murray (*left, in yellow*) entered the record books by putting Grenada 1-0 up against Honduras in 2011. It remains Grenada's only Gold Cup goal. The lead lasted just eight minutes, before Honduras roared back to win 7-1. Grenada have lost all six of their Gold Cup games, with 25 goals scored against them.

 ## THE REGGAE BOYZ

Twenty-four teams have taken part in the Gold Cup, including smaller nations such as Guadeloupe (who reached the semi-finals in 2007) and Jamaica, who had a spectacular 2015 tournament. The Reggae Boyz beat the USA in the semis to become the first Caribbean side to reach the final, where they were defeated 3-1 by Mexico.

LETHAL SCORERS

Three players have scored more than six goals at a single Gold Cup tournament. The USA's Clint Dempsey scored seven in 2015, the same tally as Mexico's Javier Hernández (*right, in green*) in 2011. Top of the table is another Mexican, Luis Roberto Alves, with 11 goals in 1993.

CONCACAF GOLD CUP CHAMPIONS

Year	Team	Year	Team
1991	USA	2005	USA
1993	Mexico	2007	USA
1996	Mexico	2009	Mexico
1998	Mexico	2011	Mexico
2000	Canada	2013	USA
2002	USA	2015	Mexico
2003	Mexico		

UNLUCKY ECUADOR

At the 2002 Gold Cup, a 2-0 victory by Ecuador over reigning champions Canada left all three Group D teams with the same number of points and equal goal difference. Lots had to be drawn to decide which two teams would progress. Haiti and Canada won and Ecuador went out of the tournament.

FIFA WOMEN'S WORLD CUP

STARS AND STRIPES

Only four teams have won the FIFA Women's World Cup, which was first held in 1991: USA (1991, 1999 and 2015), Germany (2003 and 2007), Norway (1995) and Japan (2011). The USA have never finished outside the top three, and after their 5-2 win over Japan in 2015 – the most goals in a final – are the competition's most successful side. The 2015 tournament was the third time the USA have gone through an entire Women's World Cup unbeaten.

YOUNG GUN

In 2003, Russia's Elena Danilova became the youngest goalscorer at a FIFA Women's World Cup. She was just 16 years, 96 days old when she struck against Germany in the quarter-final. The fastest goal came in 1991, scored after 30 seconds by Lena Videkull of Sweden in an 8-0 win over Japan.

Japan's captain Homare Sawa holds the FIFA Women's World Cup trophy aloft in 2011. It was Japan's first win over the USA in 26 attempts, following 22 defeats and three draws.

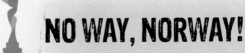

NO WAY, NORWAY!

Norway took part in the very first FIFA Women's World Cup game, losing 4-0 to hosts China. They bounced back to win their next game 4-0 versus New Zealand, and went on to score in every finals game they contested until the 1999 semi-final – a record 15-game scoring streak.

LONG-SERVING LILLY

Five players have appeared at five FIFA Women's World Cups, but Kristine Lilly has played the most games of all – a total of 30 finals matches. With 352 appearances (yielding 130 goals) for USA, Lilly is the most-capped player in world football.

QUICKFIRE CARLI

The USA's Carli Lloyd scored the fastest ever Women's World Cup hat-trick with goals in the third, fifth and 16th minutes versus Japan in the 2015 final. Her first goal was the fastest ever struck in a World Cup final and her third was the longest, with a shot from just one metre inside the halfway line. Lloyd ended the 2015 tournament as joint leading scorer with Germany's Célia Šašić, on six goals.

FIFA WOMEN'S WORLD CUP TOP SCORERS

Player	Goals
Marta (Brazil)	15
Birgit Prinz (Germany)	14
Abby Wambach (USA)	14
Michelle Akers (USA)	12
Sun Wen (China)	11
Bettina Wiegmann (Germany)	11

PART 3: Awards

Football is a team game, but some players outperform their teammates and opponents to become true matchwinners. Those who deliver exceptional performances game in, game out throughout a competition may be in line for a major award.

Some awards are voted on by professional footballers. Others are decided by judging panels of coaches, journalists and other experts, or by online fan polls. However the winner is determined, such awards are great honours and the most prestigious of all is the FIFA Ballon d'Or – awarded to the world's best footballer each year.

An all-star cast pick up their FIFA World XI awards in 2014, including (*top row left to right*) Lionel Messi, Zlatan Ibrahimović, Cristiano Ronaldo, Franck Ribéry and Xavi, and (*bottom row*) Dani Alves, Thiago Silva, Sergio Ramos, Philipp Lahm and goalkeeper Manuel Neuer.

FIFA BALLON D'OR

 ## OLDEST AND YOUNGEST

The FIFA Ballon d'Or was founded by a French football magazine in 1956 and its first winner was also its oldest. Sir Stanley Matthews picked up the trophy at the age of 41 and played in the English top division for a further nine years. In contrast, Brazilian striker Ronaldo won the award in 1997 when he was just 21.

 ## FIFA WORLD WOMEN'S PLAYER OF THE YEAR

Two players have dominated this award since its introduction in 2001. Marta won a record five times in a row (2006-10). Birgit Prinz came second to Marta in four of those years, but previously won three in a row (2003-05). All but one of the winners, which include the USA's Mia Hamm and, in 2015 and 2016, Carli Lloyd, have been attackers. In 2013, Germany's Nadine Angerer (*above right*) became the first goalkeeper to triumph, followed by German midfielder Nadine Kessler in 2014.

 ## LIONEL'S TITLES

Lionel Messi won the last original Ballon d'Or in 2009. In the following year it was merged with FIFA's World Footballer of the Year award, but the change didn't stop Messi, who went on to set a record for most wins by lifting the FIFA Ballon d'Or in 2010, 2011, 2012 and 2015. In 2013, 2014 and 2016 he finished second to Portugal's Cristiano Ronaldo.

Cristiano Ronaldo shows off the Ballon d'Or trophy. The gifted forward won the award in 2013, 2014 and 2016. In the first two of those seasons, he scored over 50 goals for Real Madrid at a rate of more than one goal per game.

TOP COACHES

The FIFA Ballon d'Or has expanded into a full awards ceremony with prizes for the best coaches and young players. Although Germany's national coach Joachim Löw (*above*) won men's coach of the year in 2014, Spanish coaches lead the awards list overall. Pep Guardiola has finished in the top three four times in six years, while the 2015 winner was Barcelona coach Luis Enrique.

REPEAT WINNERS

Besides Lionel Messi and Cristiano Ronaldo, three players have won the Ballon d'Or three times: Johan Cruyff, Michel Platini and Marco van Basten, with Platini the only one of them to win three years in a row (1983-85). Five players have won the award twice: Kevin Keegan, Ronaldo, Alfredo di Stéfano, Franz Beckenbauer and Karl-Heinz Rummenigge.

FIFA WORLD CUP AWARDS

 ## GOLDEN BALL

No player has won FIFA's World Cup award for the best player twice. Three have come close, winning and coming second in different FIFA World Cups: Pelé (1958, 1970), Paolo Rossi (1978, 1982) and Ronaldo (1998, 2002). Pelé and Ronaldo are two of seven Brazilians to win the Golden Ball – the most from any country.

 ## GOLDEN BOOT

Awarded to the highest scorer at each FIFA World Cup, no player has won this award more than once. The 1994 tournament was the last to feature more than one Golden Boot winner (Hristo Stoichkov and Oleg Salenko). Today, if tied on goals the award goes to the player with the most assists. In 2014, six goals in five matches secured Colombia's James Rodriguez (*above*) the award. Shortly after the tournament, he moved to Real Madrid for £63 million.

 ## GOLDEN GLOVES

Formerly the Yashin Award, the prize for the FIFA World Cup's best goalkeeper was first awarded to Michel Preud'Homme in 1994, despite his Belgian team being knocked out at the Round of 16 stage. All six awards have gone to European keepers, including Germany's Manuel Neuer in 2014.

WOMEN'S WORLD CUP

Similar prizes are awarded at the FIFA Women's World Cup, with US goalkeeper Hope Solo (*below right*) winning both the 2011 and 2015 Golden Gloves award. Japan's captain, Homare Sawa, scooped both best player and leading goalscorer in 2011 – a feat matched by Brazilian attacker Marta in 2007 and German striker Birgit Prinz in 2003.

Golden Gloves winner Iker Casillas makes a spectacular flying catch ahead of Robin van Persie during the 2010 FIFA World Cup final. Casillas captained his country to the title, conceding just two goals during the entire tournament.

ALL-STAR TEAM

The All-Star Team is a pick of the leading players of the tournament. Uruguay provided a record seven of the 11 players in the 1930 All-Star Team, including striker Héctor Castro who had lost his lower right arm in an accident as a teenager. Franz Beckenbauer (1966, 1970, 1974) and Djalma Santos (1954, 1958, 1962) are the only two players to feature in three All-Star Teams.

FOOTBALLER OF THE YEAR

GERMAN FOOTBALLER OF THE YEAR

This award has been given every year since 1960. The first foreign player to win was Werder Bremen's Brazilian striker Aílton Gonçalves da Silva, in 2004. Aílton's win was sandwiched between three for Bayern Munich's Michael Ballack, the last player to win a hat-trick of awards. Another Bayern player, Jérôme Boateng, won the 2016 title.

ENGLAND AND SCOTLAND

Five players have won the English PFA Player of the Year award twice: Mark Hughes, Alan Shearer, Thierry Henry, Cristiano Ronaldo and Gareth Bale. In 2017 the winner was Chelsea's N'Golo Kanté. More winners of the PFA Scottish Player of the Year award have come from Celtic than any other team – 22, including the 2017 winner, Scott Sinclair. Celtic's Henrik Larsson is the only two-time winner.

AFRICAN PLAYER OF THE YEAR

In 1992 Abedi Pele became the first winner of this award organized by the Confederation of African Football (CAF). In 2014, Manchester City and Ivory Coast's midfield powerhouse Yaya Touré (*right*) became the first player to win it four times in a row. He joins Cameroon striker Samuel Eto'o at the top of the all-time winners table, on four wins each.

⚽ NETHERLANDS AND SPAIN

HFC Haarlem's Martin Haar was the first winner of the Dutch Footballer of the Year award, in 1982. Four players have won the award twice: Frank Rijkaard, Gerald Vanenburg, Dirk Kuyt and Danny Blind. Blind's son, Daley, won in 2014, making them the first father and son winners (*below*). In Spain, six of the eight LFP Footballer of the Year awards have been won by Lionel Messi. Antoine Griezmann scooped the 2016 award.

Zlatan Ibrahimović displays his 2014 awards for the best player and best goal in France's Ligue 1. The striker has also won the Swedish Footballer of the Year award a record ten times.

⚽ FRANCE AND ITALY

The first winner of France's Player of the Year was Paris Saint-Germain's David Ginola in 1994. Another PSG player, Zlatan Ibrahimović, tops the table with wins in 2013, 2014 and 2016. Zlatan is one of only two players to win Italy's Serie A Footballer of the Year award three times, a record he shares with Andrea Pirlo. Gianluigi Buffon has dominated Serie A's Goalkeeper of the Year award (founded in 1997), winning it 11 times.

PICTURE CREDITS

The publishers would like to thank the following sources for their kind permission to reproduce the pictures in this book. The page numbers for each of the photographs are listed below, giving the page on which they appear in the book.

Key: t=top, l=left, r=right, c=centre & b=bottom.

Action Images: /Sporting Pictures: 31R

Getty Images: /AFP: 95TR; /Agence Nice Presse: 42-43; /Allsport: 106; /Gabriel Aponte/Stringer: 83TR; /The Asashi Shimbun: 74-75; /Matthew Ashton – AMA: 10-11, 116-117; /Lars Baron: 98L, 105; /Lars Baron/Bongarts: 22BL, 25; /Robyn Beck/AFP: 110-111, 117TR; /Sandra Behne/Bongarts: 81TR; /Giuseppe Bellini: 34-35; /Al Bello: 116; /John Berry: 44-45, 122; /Jorge Blanco/Latin Content: 77R; /Bongarts: 21B; /Lutz Bongarts: 67TR; /Shaun Botterill: 16-17, 66-67, 92-93; /Gabriel Bouys/AFP: 39L; /Chris Brunskill: 88-89, 91C; /Giuseppe Cacace/AFP: 36L, 36-37, 41B, 80-81; /Chung Sung-Jun: 68-69; /Robert Cianflone: 94-95; /Jean-Pierre Clatot/AFP: 49T; /Fabrice Coffrini/AFP: 120-121; /Nuno Correia: 59TR; /Helios de la Rubia/Real Madrid: 28L; /

Sebastiao de Souza/AFP: 113T; /Victor Decolongon: 72; /Adrian Dennis/AFP: 100BR; /Khaled Desouki/AFP: 114-115; /Charly Diaz Azcue/LatinContent: 82-83; /Denis Doyle: 30-31, 123L; /Fred Dufour/AFP: 47BR, 48BL; /Paul Ellis/AFP: 14BR; /Epsilon: 50-51; /Gianni Ferrari/Cover: 32L; /Franck Fife/AFP: 45TR, 109TR, 114R; /Stu Forster: 4, 101, 107B; /Stuart Franklin/Bongarts: 21TL; /Stuart Franklin/FIFA: 119T; /Quique Garcia/AFP: 28-29; /Paul Gilham: 26-27; /Laurent Gillieron/AFP: 99TR; /Laurence Griffiths: 8-9, 18-19; /Dennis Grombkowski/Bongarts: 24BL; /Gianluigi Guercia/AFP: 114B; /Valery Hache/AFP: 102-103; /Masashi Hara: 74R, 75TR; /Ronny Hartmann/AFP: 104; /Alexander Hassenstein/FIFA: 123TR; /Richard Heathcote: 16L; /Jean-Marie Hervio/AFP: 127L; /Mike Hewitt: 12-13, 91B, 100L, 125TR; /Andreas Hillergren/EuroFootball: 53TR; /Jose Jordan/AFP: 29TR; /Jasper Juinen: 30L, 62L; /Bulent Kilic/AFP: 54-55; /Andre Kosters/AFP: 57L; /Olaf Kraak/AFP: 53B; /Xavier Laine: 47L; /Oliver Lang/DDP: 65TR; /Christopher Lee: 124L; /Alex Livesey: 58, 63TR, 126; /Alexandre Loureiro: 71TL; /Juan Mabromata/AFP: 112-113; /Stuart MacFarlane: 59B; /Gabriele Maltinti: 41T; /Angel Martinez/Real Madrid: 60-61; /Masterpress: 84-85; /Jamie McDonald: 96, 108; /Buda Mendes:

70-71, 90; /Philippe Merle/AFP: 48-49; /Aris Messinis/AFP: 52; /Olivier Morin/AFP: 39R, 62-63; /Beate Mueller/Bongarts: 40; /Mark Nolan/Stringer: 76; /Ryan Pierse: 86-87; /New Press: 38; /Martin Peters/Manchester United: 67L; /Plumb Images/Leicester City FC: 14-15; /Joern Pollex: 109B; /Anne-Christine Poujoulat/AFP: 44L; /Andrew Powell/Liverpool FC: 17TR; /Dani Pozo/AFP: 33; /Cristina Quicler/AFP: 32BR; /Ben Radford: 94L; /David Rogers: 57TR; /Miguel Rojo/AFP: 77L; /Rolls Press/Popperfoto: 22T; /Clive Rose: 15TR, 124-125; /Miguel Ruiz/FC Barcelona: 64-65; /Jamie Sabau: 72-73; /Miguel Schincariol/AFP: 82BL; /Antonio Scorza/AFP: 70L, 97B; /Ben Stanshall: 1; /Michael Steele: 92L; /Patrik Stollarz/AFP: 97T, 98-99, 118-119; /Boris Streubel: 23; /Bob Thomas: 24R; /Mark Thompson: 14L; /John Thys/AFP: 64; /VI-Images: 55TR, 56, 107T, 127R; /Visionhaus: 2, 81TR; /Angelika Warmuth/AFP: 20-21; /Jim Watson/AFP: 12L; /Thomas Wirth/AFP: 46; /Andrew Yates/AFP: 13C; /Zhong Zhi: 78-79

Every effort has been made to acknowledge correctly and contact the source and/or copyright holder of each picture and Carlton Books Limited apologises for any unintentional errors or omissions that will be corrected in future editions of this book.